D0614262

SEPTEMBER 11

A MEMOIR

SEPTEMBER 11

A MEMOIR

Never forget !
William Groneman III

William Groneman III

Captain (retired), Engine Company 308
Fire Department of the City of New York

GOLDMINDS

NASHVILLE, TENNESSEE

Goldminds Publishing, LLC.
1050 Glenbrook Way, Suite 480
Hendersonville, TN 37075

September 11: A Memoir

Copyright © William Groneman III, August 2011.

ISBN 13: 978-1-930584-39-6

Cover photo copyright © Lt. John Leavy, courtesy of the Fire
Department of the City of New York.
Author photo copyright © Liz and Joe Schmidt Photography, Inc.

Printed in the United States of America

Without limiting the rights under the copyright reserved above, no part
of this publication may be reproduced, stored in or introduced into a
retrieval system, or transmitted, in any form or by any means
(electronic, mechanical, photocopying, recording or otherwise), without
the prior written permission of both the copyright owner and the above
publisher of this book.

www.goldmindspub.com

This book is dedicated to the Brothers and Sisters of the Fire Department of the City of New York. Especially the 343.

ACKNOWLEDGEMENTS

I sincerely thank the following:

Jean (Ma) and Mikey Novak for their assistance in getting this project in print. Steve Law, good friend from the Western Writers of America (WWA), and Goldminds Publishing. Ryan Crawford and the team at Goldminds. Nancy Plain, award winning writer, also of WWA who kindly offered her considerable proof-reading skills. Kirk and Sheila Ellis of WWA. Kirk's interest in part one of this memoir last year inspired me to bring it to completion. In fact I thank all of my extended family in the WWA for their encouragement.

A number of people generously provided photographs and permission to use them: Director Stephen Paul Antonelli, and Productions Manager Thomas Ittycheria of FDNY Publications; FDNY Assistant Council Tayo Kurzman; and Deputy Commissioner Francis X. Gribbon. Gerald and Joyce Cereghino. Gerald was on the scene at

Ground Zero, providing and supervising heavy equipment in the rescue effort. He also captured some unique photographs. Finally Steve Spak, *the* photographer of New York City fire and emergency scenes for many years.

I thank the guys from Engine Company 308 and Battalion 51. It was a pleasure to have served with them, and to have completed my career with them: Lieutenants Joe Mills, Cliff Payan, Bob Urso. Firefighters Tom McAllister, Tony Bonfiglio, Steve George, Gregg Lawrence, Chris Simmons, Craig Moore, Wayne Slater, John Ostrick, Bob O'Hara, Kevin Crosby, Randy Rodrigues, Jimmy Ferretti, Mark Presti, Tom Gathmann, Paul Sokol, Al Merk, Joe Gick, Phil Lanasa, and Tom Lynch. The probationary firefighters who were detailed in at the time, Matt Swan, John Barone, and Brian Cross, and those who were detailed out, Steve Cox, Jim Moody, Steve Kelly, and Terry McShane (rest in peace). From the Battalion: Chiefs Thomas Narbutt, Ken Grabowski, and Mike Borst, and firefighters Ralph Scerbo, Joe McCormack, Ralph Nichols and Johnny Mazzullo. I also want to single out Joe Gick, Mark Presti, Randy Rodrigues, and Chris Simmons who provided some last minute fine-tuning of facts.

Finally, I thank Kelly, daughter Katie, son Billy and brother Michael. They were there and went through it all from the beginning. Thanks for helping me through dark days.

And, I thank Weimaraner Brooklyn Dodger Groneman for keeping me company while I wrote and typed.

INTRODUCTION

I began writing this account on September 11, 2003. It is an account of my experiences on September 11, 2001, during the terrorist attack on America, and in the weeks and months following. Originally I wrote down some experiences and observations about ten days after the attack but never followed it up to completion. I started again in 2003 so I would have a record of what I did and observed that day. Much time had passed already and there was the danger of too many little details being lost or forgotten. I believe that anyone who was a witness to the attack on the World Trade Center or the Pentagon or to Flight 93 in Pennsylvania should write down their memories of the event in detail in order that a living history is preserved for the future. I also realize that this may be impossible for many since their experiences were too traumatic. This is not to say that I did anything outstanding or noteworthy. I did not. I was just a very small player in a very big drama.

Some things may have been lost. Outside influences may have affected my memory of things. Comparing my reminiscences to someone else's, even someone who was right beside me, could reveal discrepancies. As John

Steinbeck wrote in *Travels With Charley,* "[T]he memory is at best a faulty, warpy reservoir."

I attempted a follow-up to this original record beginning writing on September 11, 2007, but never got past the title. I revised my original in July, 2010, in order to tighten it up and remove much of which was repetitive. Part I is my revision of the original. Part II is what happened afterwards.

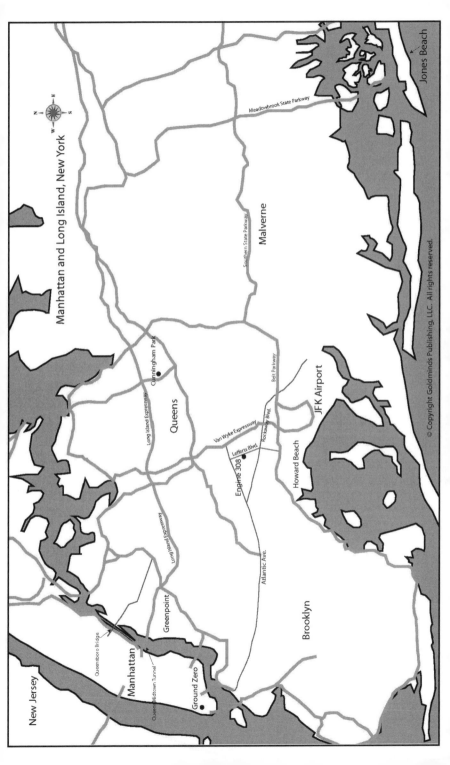

Manhattan and Long Island, New York

New Jersey

Manhattan

Queensboro Bridge

Queens Midtown Tunnel

Ground Zero

Greenpoint

Long Island Expressway

Long Island Expressway

Cunningham Park

Queens

Brooklyn

Atlantic Ave.

Engine 308

Lefferts Blvd.

Van Wyck Expressway

Rockaway Blvd.

Howard Beach

Belt Parkway

JFK Airport

Southern State Parkway

Malverne

Meadowbrook State Parkway

Jones Beach

© Copyright Goldminds Publishing, LLC. All rights reserved.

PART I

TUESDAY MORNING

OMENS AND PORTENTS

I was a captain of the Fire Department of the City of New York (hereafter FDNY) in 2001. I had been assigned as company commander of Engine Company 308, Battalion 51, Division 13, in the borough of Queens the year before. I had twenty-four years on the job at the time, previously having served in the ranks of firefighter, fire marshal, and lieutenant.

A few things happened during the spring and summer of 2001 that seemed unremarkable at the time. One was the demolition of two oil storage tanks in the Greenpoint section of Brooklyn during the spring. These two large tanks had been a part of the New York City landscape for years. If one watches the film *The Godfather* these tanks are visible in the background during the cemetery scene of Vito Corleone's funeral. They were imploded during the spring of 2001 in a much publicized event. Many members of the FDNY were present as the two tanks collapsed.

A few weeks prior to September 11, my daughter Katie and I attended a party at a friend's home in Pennsylvania. The party was some distance from our home on Long Island so we stayed overnight at a hotel in Pennsylvania. As we drove through Patterson, New Jersey, on the ride home the following morning I noticed a flock of birds flying frantically from left to right across Route 80, maybe fifty to seventy-five feet up. Suddenly two birds detached themselves from the rest, plunged down and smashed into my windshield. I have no idea why that happened but I had never seen anything like that before or since.

Besides working in my own fire company, I also worked a special assignment once a week at FDNY headquarters in Brooklyn. Fire Commissioner Thomas Von Essen had asked me to write an article for our magazine *WNYF (With New York Firefighters)* about the changes in the FDNY under Mayor Rudolph Giuliani. I had helped bring this magazine back into print after a two year hiatus a few years before and then served as its technical editor. I left headquarters late on Monday, two weeks prior to September 11, walking through the lobby and passing the Memorial Wall. The Wall is on the left-hand side as you leave the lobby. It is made up of small bronze plaques with the name, rank, company, and date of death of all members of the FDNY who had died in the line of duty since the FDNY became a paid department in 1865. As I was leaving I noticed Commissioner Von Essen, First Deputy Commissioner William Feehan, Chief of Department Peter Ganci, civilian Roy Katz, in charge of Fire Department buildings, and maybe one or two others gathered at the wall and discussing something. At the time there were 782 names on the wall and only room for about six or eight more. It later occurred to me that they were discussing how to increase the size of the wall in order to accommodate more names in the future.[1]

One week later I stood in the lobby after lunch with Steve Antonelli, a civilian employee of the department with whom I worked. He looked at the wall and asked me if a chief officer had ever been killed in the line of duty, or who was the last chief killed. I answered immediately that the last chief killed was Battalion Chief Frank Tuttlemundo of Battalion 44, in 1980. I remembered that because at the time I was a firefighter in Engine 332, in the East New York section of Brooklyn, and often we would respond to the same alarms as Battalion 44.[2]

At the time none of these occurrences had any significance. After, and taken all together, they did seem a bit strange.

SEPTEMBER 11, 2001

I had worked in Engine 308, in the Richmond Hill section of Queens on Sunday night, September 9, from 6:00 p.m. to 9:00 a.m. Monday morning. In FDNY parlance this is known as the night tour, the "six by nine," or simply "the six-by." That Monday morning I left the firehouse and traveled to FDNY headquarters, at 9 MetroTech Center in the downtown section of Brooklyn, to work on the article about the Fire Department under the Giuliani administration. I traveled from the firehouse to headquarters by subway—eleven stops on the A Train.

Nothing remarkable happened during the night tour at firehouse or at headquarters. It was merely business as usual. As I left headquarters late on Monday afternoon I passed the Memorial Wall, as mentioned above, and returned to the firehouse via the A Train. Things were quiet at the firehouse. I changed into civilian clothes, put my work duty uniform from the night before into my bag to bring home to wash, and left for the ten mile drive to my home in Malverne, Long Island.

September 11, 2001, was a beautiful day. It probably was one of the ten best weather days of the year. There had been a storm out over the ocean the day before and it gave everything a clean and fresh look. The air was warm and the sky clear blue with a few high clouds. My daughter, Katie, a fourth grader at Maurice W. Downing School, had gone back to school a week earlier. My wife, Kelly, was president of the Downing PTA and also a substitute teacher at the school. The school was only one block from our house. That morning Kelly presided over a PTA meeting at the school.

Since I had nothing pressing to do I decided to go out to Jones Beach State Park, about fifteen miles east on the south shore of Long Island, for a walk and jog along the boardwalk and beach. Jones Beach is a beautiful beach which holds many fond memories. My father would take my brother and me there when we were children to swim in the ocean or in the large saltwater pool. I started to go out there on my own when I was a senior in high school. It is one of my favorite places in the world. I had been taking every opportunity to go there. We had plans to move to Texas after I retired, and, since I would be "land-locked" within the next year and a half, the beach became increasingly precious to me.

Kelly did not need her car, a white Jeep Grande Cherokee, to go to school so I took it to Jones Beach rather than my own 1992 Chevy Cavalier. My Cavalier, known in FDNY slang as my "ghetto car," was the one I took to work. It was in less than pristine condition, having suffered the wear and tear of traveling to, and being parked outside of, New York City firehouses for nine years. The air conditioner and cassette player no longer worked. Naturally the Jeep was a more comfortable ride. I took the jeep with Kelly's blessing and headed out.

JONES BEACH

Jones Beach is probably less than fifteen miles from Malverne. One takes the Southern State Parkway eastbound to the Meadowbrook Parkway southbound which leads directly into Jones Beach. Malverne is at exit 17 on the Southern State Parkway and the Meadowbrook is at exit 22. It is the quickest route to Jones Beach, but not on the morning of September 11, 2001. I entered the Southern State and found, to my dismay, bumper-to-bumper traffic going east. I never could figure out why the Southern State was like this toward the end of the rush hour on a weekday morning. If anything, the westbound traffic toward New York City should be moving slowly. I immediately regretted taking this route and not taking the alternate route via Sunrise Highway (with traffic lights) to the south and then onto the Meadowbrook. However, I reminded myself to relax and enjoy the morning. I merged into the slowly moving traffic and put the radio on. Normally I switch the radio back and forth between one or two jazz stations, a classical station, and an all-news station while driving in my own car. It is a force of habit that while driving in New York City I constantly switch to the all-news WINS, that gives traffic reports every ten minutes. On this morning I conceded the fact that I was already in traffic, that it was too late to do anything about it, and that I was on my way to Jones Beach anyway. Since I had the luxury of a working cassette player I forgot about WINS, put on a tape of Bach, and relaxed to the strains of *Jesu, the Joy of Man's Desiring*, and other Bach pieces.

Traffic was heavy until I reached the Meadowbrook, then I sailed south on this road, past the toll booths, over the draw bridge crossing the State Boat Channel, onto Ocean Drive and into Jones Beach. Normally I park in Parking Field 4, northwest of Jones Beach's landmark water tower. I either park on the west or east end of the parking lot and enter the beach area by way of the tunnels that go under Ocean Drive. If I want a short run or walk I park on the west side. If I want a slightly longer trek I park on the east side. In either case I travel west on the boardwalk to Parking Field 1 and then back along the shore line. On this particular morning I decided to maximize my time there and parked in Parking Field 6, the easternmost field on the ocean side. I had never done this before, and I do not know why I did it this morning. It is not all that much farther, but a walk from there encompasses all of Jones Beach.

I parked in Parking Field 6 sometime between 8:30 and 8:45 a.m. Later, I determined it probably was closer to 8:30, for reasons that will be explained. The parking field was not crowded. I parked near the concession stand with the jeep facing toward the exit. As was my habit I brought a cell phone, a small towel, and a small cooler with me. The cooler contained a bottle of Gatorade, and one or two small fist-sized bottles of water. I always carried one of the water bottles on the run/walk. I left the phone and towel. I locked the Jeep, did some leg stretches against the rear bumper, set my wrist watch to stop-watch mode, and headed west on the board walk.

The area near the concession stand of Field 6 is a gathering place for the over sixty crowd. This morning was no different. The regulars were in their beach chairs or at the picnic tables, having their coffee and chatting. I passed them and went on my way.

It had been my habit for years to recite the Rosary to myself while jogging. I never carried a set of Rosary beads with me but counted the prayers off on my fingers. Afterwards I say the Prayer to Saint Joseph nine times. I then recite the poem "The Beaks of Eagles" by Robinson Jeffers. It is about the Big Sur Country of California's central coast and the only poem I know by heart. I followed the established pattern that morning.

I alternated by walking and running since I was just trying to get back into a regular running routine. According to an account I wrote ten days later I walked for ten minutes, ran for five, walked for another five, and then ran for five again.

The boardwalk at Jones Beach is a beautiful well-kept walk of wood. At some places along the path, such as in the areas of the East and West Bathhouses or near parking fields, the wood ends and one passes over concrete. The concrete areas are linked by the wooden boardwalks. There are a number of leisure and sports activities on the north side of the walk between the East and West Bathhouses.

I was struck by a wave of nostalgia as I passed each of these activities. Each station along the way brought a pleasant memory about different people and different stages of my life. I did not dwell on it then, except to enjoy each of these memories. Later, when I reflected on events it seemed as if these thoughts, as well as the whole peaceful time at the beach, served as an interlude between the pre- and post-9/11 worlds.

I noticed the second-floor gallery of the East Bathhouse that overlooks the boardwalk and ocean as I passed by. I thought back to when I sat in one of the chairs up there in 1997 and wrote the introduction to my book *Battlefields of Texas*, which was published a year later.[3] Next I passed the basketball courts and remembered fondly that just a couple of week earlier Kelly, Katie, and I had a good time shooting some baskets there. Next was a pitch-and-putt golf course. I smiled as I recalled that on the day after Katie was born (she was born on July 15, 1992), I brought my son Billy (15 years old at the time) here and we golfed a round. Billy teed off on one hole. The ball bounced twice, hit the pin and went right in the hole. I went nuts, jumping around yelling, "A hole in one! A hole in one!" and pointing at Billy. He was embarrassed but we had a few laughs over it later.

The Boardwalk Restaurant on the Central Mall came next. I had eaten there a few times in the past, but not in years. It has since been taken down and I do not know what has been put up in its place. There is a large flagpole in the middle of the Central Mall in the design of a ship's mast. Beyond that as you look to the right toward Ocean Drive is Jones Beach's most identifiable landmark, the Water Tower. It is a huge structure and looks like a brick, art-deco rocket ship. There is a snack stand across the Central Mall from the restaurant where Katie and I often stopped for totally unhealthy hot dogs and fries. Katie loved to feed the sea gulls at the beach. I remembered a time we were eating in the snack stand and she could not wait to get back outside with her hot dog bun and give it to the gulls. I finally said she could go out and she took off running, hunched over with her nose pointing forward, totally focused on her mission. A small band shell and then a miniature golf course come after the snack stand. I took Billy and then Katie to play miniature golf there when they were younger. Each hole on this course has a wooden model (a boat, a lighthouse, a building, etc.) representing a different New York State Park on Long Island. Next are shuffleboard and paddleball courts. My father took my brother and me to these when we were young.

A fairly new playground is on the right, just before one reaches the West Bathhouse. It is a modern one of wood and plastic. I took Katie there on many mornings when she was off from school, regardless of the season. She would climb, slide, and swing on the different devices while I sat on one of the wooden benches working on some current writing project. However, at her persistence I always ended up chasing her around the playground while she screamed and laughed and eluded me. I remembered that a few years earlier we had even come out here on New Year's Day—and froze. Years ago when I was Katie's age there was an archery range in this area. My father would take us there too.

The West Bathhouse is the main building of Jones Beach. It houses a large saltwater open-air swimming pool. There is an ice-cream parlor on the second floor and another snack bar on the first. This is another place I had come many times with my father. Later, when I was in college, it became the official hang-out for me and my friend Ed DeCastro. We came to the beach to body surf, which usually meant getting pummeled by the waves. We would always go into the ocean three separate times. On one of the breaks in between we went to the snack stand for our "official meal"—a cheeseburger, fries, and either a 7-Up or root beer float (a soda with a large dollop of Carvel ice cream).

All of these memories played themselves out as I walked and ran along. It was the only time I had ever connected with these memories for the whole distance of the Jones Beach boardwalk, and I never remembered having such a nostalgic feel for everything.

West of the West Bathhouse there are no other games or leisure activities along the boardwalk except for an old Softball East Field between the bathhouse and Parking Field 2, and a new Softball West Field between Parking Fields 2 and 1. There are fewer people along this stretch of boardwalk. Sand dunes covered with a variety of coastline grasses and plants obscure the view of the ocean along this stretch. Things are more peaceful up at this end.

There are a few roofed-over shaded areas with backless concrete benches on the ocean side along the boardwalk. I usually stop and do a set of thirty push-ups on some of these benches while doing my walk/run. I do some more down near the water on the way back, trying to do at least 120 total. One of these shaded areas is located where the boardwalk resumes, just west of the West Bathhouse. There is another one a short distance just west of this one. I do not remember at which one I stopped, but I know that I did push-ups at one of them. I know I finished 120 before returning to my car. I probably did the rest on the sand.

WITNESS UNAWARE

I happened to look toward the west at some points between Fields 1 and 2 and saw what appeared to be a mushroom cloud on the horizon. I thought to myself, facetiously, that Japan had gotten revenge for World War II by A-bombing New Jersey. I did not stop to look at it but kept on walking and running. I glanced at it maybe three times. It looked like a grey vertical column with a cloud evenly around its top. In reality I thought it probably was a large fire somewhere in the boroughs of Queens or Brooklyn. I thought that the vertical column was the smoke rising and that some atmospheric phenomenon caused the smoke to spread out at a certain point. I also thought that somewhere the Brothers (New York City Firefighters) were having a good time fighting a large fire. I must have looked at it one last time before reaching the eastern edge of Parking Field 1. Trees around the field would have blocked my view from that point on. It never occurred to me that I was looking at the World Trade Center for the last time. Only 15 to 20 minutes had passed since I started my trek. The first hijacked plane is said to have hit One World Trade Center at 8:46 a.m. I believe that I saw Tower One with the smoke around the top within minutes, if not seconds, after the first plane hit. Later on I saw films and photos in which the smoke from the top of the Tower trailed off like the blade of a scythe. It did not yet look like that when I saw it. This reasoning leads me to believe that I arrived at Parking Field 6 some time around 8:30 a.m.

I walked to the end of the concrete walk at Field 1, following my usual routine, symbolically stepped off into the sand at the end, did an about face and walked a short distance back to a bench. There I removed my sneakers and sweat socks, put the socks in one of the sneakers, the water bottle in the other, and then tied the sneakers together through loops on the back of each with a small piece of clothes line I carried. I hung the sneakers over my shoulder and walked down to the water. The beach is wide here and it takes a good five minutes to reach the water. Walking is a little slower in the access path between the dunes because the sand is soft and deep, but it felt good on the feet. There are always tire tracks of beach maintenance vehicles in this area. Signs warn to stay off the dunes and to be aware that endangered plovers nest in the dunes and sometimes in the tire tracks.

I removed my shirt and probably did another set of thirty push-ups when I reached the water line, and then spent a few minutes there. The beach is usually deserted at this end and the sense of remoteness is enjoyable. I have rarely seen anyone else in this area. Depending on conditions such as the tide, recent storms, etc., the walking here can be easy or difficult. Sometimes the sand near the water is packed down and as firm as a roadway. Other times it can be soft and on a slope. I do not remember what conditions were that day. The waves were pretty big and breaking with a majestic regularity due to the storm the day before.

I started on my way back east, with the sun in my face and enjoying the salt spray from the waves. I probably stopped to do push-ups once or twice more since this would have been my normal routine. I do not remember seeing too many people. I may have seen a lone surf-caster fishing around the area of Field 2. Usually I take my time and savor the solitude but that morning I began to get a feeling that my walk was taking too long. I also began to get a feeling that I had to get back, even though there was no reason to do so. The feeling at the time was almost like a clamp on the back of my neck. I had not recognized the World Trade Center with the cloud of smoke around it earlier, but something may have kicked in subliminally, telling me something was very wrong.

A group of surfers stood near the water in the area of the West Bathhouse. This in itself was unusual since surfing is not allowed here during the regular summer season. However, this was after Labor Day. One surfer was in the water on his board out where the waves were breaking. With him in perspective I could get a pretty good idea of how big the waves were. They were good-sized waves and looked perfect for surfing. To my left and in the vicinity of the main lifeguard stand was one girl and three or four guys all in their black wet suits and with their boards. I could not understand why they were not in the water since the waves were so good. They had a portable radio with them and were standing around it talking. I could not hear the radio or what they were talking about. I had the impression that their conversation was light-hearted. This was based on nothing other than what else would surfers' conversation be, at the beach on a beautiful morning with great waves. I passed them and turned around to see if the guy in the water had caught any waves. He had not. I continued on but the fact that all the surfers were not in the water still seemed strange to me.

Nothing else unusual happened during the rest of the walk back. I reached the beach area of Field 6, stopped for a moment and took one last look at the ocean, put on my shirt and went back toward the parking field.

A section of wooden boardwalk comes out per-pendicular to the main boardwalk between the East Bathhouse and Field 6. It is probably 25' to 30' long. I did not take this walk while returning from the water but maximized my time on the sand. I reached the main boardwalk just west of Parking Field 6. I stopped my stop watch and noticed that I had taken exactly one hour and twenty minutes to complete the whole circuit. This would have made it about 9:50 a.m. This is one time interval I can be sure of that day. I made a mental note of it because I usually spend no more than an hour on these morning beach jaunts.

I sat on a bench, dusted the sand from my feet and put on my socks and sneakers. I probably had finished the small bottle of water by then. I was not aware of anything unusual as I walked past the building with the snack bar, but I had a vague feeling that people were quieter than usual, not that the older crowd was ever that noisy anyhow. It also seemed that some people were standing around in close groups talking, but I really did not pay much attention to them. I was almost to the edge of the parking field when I noticed an older woman sitting in a beach chair on the sand, right near the cement area of the snack stand. She was to my right and facing in my direction. I noticed her because she sat there with a sort of strange, disassociated smile on her face. There was a portable radio in front of her and it was on.

The sense of urgency in the radio commentator's voice caught my attention. I could not make out all that he said, but I remember five words very clearly. "Disaster... Mayor Giuliani... Thousands dead!"

THE RIDE

I sprinted to the jeep without waiting to hear more. The thought of a horrible accident on one of the New York City Subway lines flashed through my mind. However, this did not seem to click. A disaster on the subway during rush hour had the potential of causing hundreds of deaths and/or injuries. I could not imagine what could have cause *thousands* of deaths. I hopped into the jeep, turned on the ignition and radio, and probably went right to the all news WINS. Immediately it reported that a plane had gone into

web site www.WGroneman.com

email wgroneman@yahoo.com

830-285-8646

ter. I finally realized that the
een *was* the World Trade Center.

izy at this point. I felt as if I was
and planning actions on about six
time planes had hit the both towers
iter. American Airlines flight 11 hit
a.m., and United Airlines flight 175
9:03 a.m. I know that I must have
but I have no clear memory of it. I
aware that it was a terrorist attack
saying to myself, "This is Pearl
e Pearl Harbor!"

ghts came very rapidly. I felt that all
t morning was a thing in the distant
r to be retrieved. I felt a strong
nostalgia for the past which was anything five minutes ago.
There was a sensation of having passed through a portal to
another world. Everything was changed right at that split
second. There also was a strange feeling of relief that is
difficult to explain. It was as if we had always been moving
toward this moment, now it finally was here, and we could
stop worrying about when it would come. Now we just had
to deal with it.

Personally I had the feeling of a great weight being
lifted from me. Everyone has any number of things on his
or her mind causing concern and anxiety on a daily basis—
problems with houses, cars, family, money, etc. I was no
different, with concerns about our impending move,
building a new house, selling a house, retirement, and other
things. Suddenly these were all lifted from my shoulders.
Now the only thing that mattered was getting to work and
staying alive. Life was broken down to its barest essentials.
I knew I had to get to the firehouse, but I also had the

thought that I had to take care of my family. A strange idea went through my mind as I tried to figure out the best course of action. I thought, "It doesn't matter—we're all dead already!" This thought repeated itself a number of times during the day.

I tried to call the firehouse a couple of times before I left the parking lot but could not get through. I also tried to call home, with no luck. Cursing, I gave up and concentrated on driving. While leaving the parking lot another thought occurred to me. I knew what I had to do as a member of the Fire Department. Also, as somewhat of an historian and writer, I had to try to remember everything I saw that day so I would be able to tell others or set it down for history's sake. This would prove easier said than done. I remember one other crazy thought at the time, that the United States had to take over the whole world and that the rest of the planet should live or die at the whim of the United States.

The exit from Parking Field 6 puts you on Ocean Drive, eastbound. I drove the few hundred feet to a turn-around and headed west, back toward the Meadowbrook Parkway. I was able to get a quick glance to the west while on the drawbridge over the State Boat Channel. One can see the skyscrapers of midtown and downtown silhouetted on the horizon on a clear day from this bridge. However, all of downtown was obscured by a tremendous cloud of smoke that stretched south over the entrance to New York Harbor by this time. Normally if I had seen something as shocking as this I would have slowed down and done some rubbernecking. Now, I just gave a look to my left and imprinted the image on my mind. I thought to myself, "Don't bother looking. You're going to get a lot closer before the night is over."

I drove in the left lane as fast as I had ever driven, hitting speeds of 90 miles per hour. I flashed my headlights and blew the horn. I tried to follow what was being said on the radio but cannot remember most of it. I do remember that a short time after I had crossed the drawbridge the news reported that one of the towers had collapsed. This sticks in my mind because I started to scream at the top of my lungs. I could not fathom the number of people who may have been killed.

I drove as fast as I could. While on the merge to enter the Southern State Parkway I had the sensation of the jeep's right wheels leaving the ground. Traffic was moderately heavy but moving. I weaved in and out, with horn blaring and lights flashing, driving so aggressively that I was back in Malverne in no time. I roared up Nassau Avenue screeching to a stop in front of my house. Kelly came running out before I was out of the jeep. We ran back and forth past one another two or three times while yelling things at one another. She said that the firehouse called and there was a total recall. I answered "I know," without having any way of knowing that. I just assumed it would be so. A "Total Recall" means that every off-duty member of the FDNY is called back to duty.

I ran into the house to get the keys to my car. I also got the bag with my uniform from Sunday which I had never washed. I saw the TV as I was going out the front door that showed a film of the second plane plowing into Tower Two. I caught a glimpse but did not even stop to watch. Kelly asked me if I wanted her to iron my unwashed uniform shirt. This struck me as funny because it reminded me of a scene in Walter Lord's, *Day of Infamy,* a book about the Japanese attack on Pearl Harbor. Lord described Master Sergeant Arthur Fahrner frantically dressing to rush out to battle. While he did this his wife kept handing him a tie. Finally Fahrner told her, "We're at war. You don't wear a tie to war." We were at war. I had several other sets of work-duty uniforms at the firehouse, so I probably didn't need the uniform I had with me. However, I did not know how long I would be gone and I wanted everything I had available to me.

I switched to my car, the Chevy Cavalier, for a couple of reasons. I wanted Kelly to have her Jeep because it was newer and sturdier in case she and Katie had to get out of there. I wanted my car because I did not know what conditions would be within the city limits. If I had to ditch the older car somewhere—who cared? I bid Kelly good-bye and told her to take care of Katie, telling her that I probably would not be home for about four days. Why four days? Who knows? I told her that I would call if I could since I had my cell phone with me. In a moment of insanity before entering my car I cursed all terrorists yelling that I was going to quit the Fire Department after this was over, join the Marine Corps, and kill these bastards. After my rant I took off down the block, heading for the Southern State Parkway again.

Hempstead Avenue is the main street in Malverne. One takes this north to get on the Southern State Parkway west toward New York City, going around a "clover leaf" type entrance ramp. I did this and immediately saw that traffic was stopped on the three lane highway. A New York State Trooper's car blocked the middle of the parkway just beyond the overpass I had just come over. The trooper was out of his car, stopping all traffic to the city and directing it up onto Hempstead Avenue. I knew that this would not apply to emergency service workers. So I looked for some quick way to identify myself. I grabbed a placard from my union, the Uniformed Fire Officers Association. It states that the bearer is a Fire Officer on official business. It is virtually useless in the city other than for parking in a fire zone outside a firehouse while one is working. Today, it was gold. I made eye contact with a woman in a car in the left lane and showed her the card. She let me squeeze into the lane in front of her. I held the card up in the windshield as I inched towards the trooper and noticed that guys in other cars were holding up badges and baseball caps with FDNY or NYPD on them. The trooper looked at each one and then waved them on. When my time finally came I took off as fast as the Cavalier could handle, towards New York City.

I accelerated steadily, probably reaching 90 miles per hour but that did not last long. I had entered the parkway at exit 17. There is a small New York State Troopers' station on the westbound side, just near exit 13. A tall black trooper, whom I had often seen patrolling this area, had traffic halted. Once again firefighters and police officer lined up in the left lane, identified themselves, and waited for their turns. The trooper looked carefully at each piece of identification and then waved on the car with one quick jerk of his right hand. There were two or three cars ahead of me. Normally when waiting in traffic a driver may be fidgety, impatient, and may look all around. I did not even look around to see if I knew anyone in the other cars. I sat there hunched over the steering wheel, with my hands in a death grip in the 2 and 10 o'clock positions, and my eyes riveted on the trooper. He gave me the signal and I floored it.

There was no traffic at this point except for emergency service workers racing along, but once again that was short-lived. The border line between Nassau County, in which I lived, and Queens County (one of New York City's five boroughs) is only about a mile or so west of the State Troopers' station. Traffic was at its moderate mid-morning volume just over the city limits. The Southern State Parkway becomes the Laurelton Parkway in Queens, going south for a few miles and then turning into the Belt Parkway, going west again. I continued to weave in and out of traffic with my lights and horn going. At all times since I had gotten on the Southern State, but especially on high overpasses, I could see the tremendous cloud of smoke from Lower Manhattan.

I followed the route I usually took to work, staying on the Belt Parkway and taking the exit ramp for the Van Wyke Expressway going north. This is practically right at the entrance to Kennedy Airport, which is south on Van Wyke.

I stayed on the service road and made a left onto 133rd Avenue, which goes through the neighborhood of South Ozone Park. It is a narrow, hilly street, lined with old wood-frame houses. I sped along, driving much too fast for this street. I only slowed once and that was for sentimental reasons. Every time I drove into work along this route I slowed down while crossing 124th Street and looked to my left at the small house in which my father was raised. I did it every time, so I did it this time. I hoped that my father, and Grandma and Grandpa Groneman, and my mother's parents, Grandma and Grandpa DeLaurenzo were looking down on me and would help me get through this day.

Enough sentimentality. I hit the gas again, racing the few blocks to Lefferts Boulevard, but not stopping for the red light. I made a right, putting me northbound on Lefferts, which would take me right to Engine 308. Lefferts is four lanes wide at this point but narrows to two lanes north of Rockaway Boulevard. Traffic is usually slow moving. The closer I got to the firehouse the more frantically I drove. At one point I drove against oncoming traffic in the opposite lane, still flashing headlights and blowing the horn. I slowed for a red light at Rockaway Blvd., then shot across four lanes against the light. Looking to the left as I crossed Rockaway Blvd., I could see the horrific cloud boiling up from Lower Manhattan. I raced the last two blocks and roared up onto the apron of Engine Company 308's quarters.

THE FIREHOUSE

The firehouse's apparatus door was opened. A group of firefighters gathered around the house watch desk, intently listening to the department radio. As soon as I got out of the car I smelled something burning and realized that it was my car. A few of the guys drifted over. I heard someone say, "What's that burning?" and another, I think it was John Ostrick deadpanned, "It's the Captain's brakes." I thought no more about it. If the car caught on fire, it was right outside the firehouse.

Bob Urso, the lieutenant on duty, walked toward me, and I asked him for a rundown. By this time I had come to the knowledge that both towers had collapsed. I must have heard it on the radio on the ride in. Bob probably repeated that information, and when I acknowledged it he said in a quiet, emotion-strained voice, "You don't understand. There was a Fifth Alarm assignment—in each of the buildings." I let the information sink in.

The guys around the house watch desk were listening to transmission over the department radio from Captain Al

Fuentes of the Marine Division (Fire Boats), who was trapped in debris at the scene. We thought that Al was trapped in a department vehicle since he was communicating with the dispatcher via the department radio. Actually, he had a special handi-talkie that allowed him to communicate over the department radio frequency. He was later rescued.[4]

I moved my car off the apron and squeezed into a parking space near the firehouse. Most New York City firehouses are home to two companies—an engine and a ladder company. In some instances an engine company shares the house with one of the city's five rescue companies. There are a few firehouses which are home to three companies but these are rare. Engine 308 is what is considered a "single" engine company in that there is no ladder or rescue company housed in the same quarters. It does share quarters with Battalion 51. Engine 308 is one of four engine companies and two ladder companies that make up Battalion 51, or in FDNY parlance "The Five-One." The battalion office is on the second floor of the firehouse, as is Engine 308's office. A small locker room for the engine officers, separates the offices. Battalion Chief Thomas Narbutt was the battalion commander at the time. Besides Chief Narbutt there were two other regularly assigned battalion chiefs, and perhaps one covering chief, as well as firefighters assigned as the chief's aides. Each chief is supposed to have his own aide, but the battalion may have been short at the time. Often Engine 308 would detail a firefighter to the battalion on any given tour to act as aide.

I went upstairs and stopped in the battalion office. There may have been a number of people there. I only remember Battalion Chief Ken Grabowski. I asked him what we were supposed to do. He told me that Cunningham

Park in Queens had been set up as a staging area for Division 13, our division, and that we were supposed to go there. I went into the locker room and changed into my uniform. There is a supply closet inside the locker room. I looked in there for any spare tools, such as Halligan tools, axes, hooks, or shovels that we could take with us. I found that the closet had already been stripped of all spare tools, as had been the rest of the firehouse. I returned to the apparatus floor and went into the kitchen at the rear. I cannot remember who was in the kitchen at the time or what happened, but I do remember the image of the second plane plowing into Tower Two being shown on the television. Back on the apparatus floor I collected my gear, consisting of bunker pants and boots, bunker coat, gloves, and helmet from the engine officer's closet. I brought these to the front and piled them on the floor in front of the engine.

I believe that some of the guys had assembled and started for the staging area already. They must have because someone had taken all of the spare tools. I assembled the first five guys who were ready to go with me. They were Jimmy Ferretti, Al Merk, Nick D'Onofrio, John Ostrick, and Ralph Scerbo. Jimmy Ferretti, Al Merk, and Nick D'Onofrio were all senior men. They all were regular engine company chauffeurs (ECCs), which means that they all were assigned to work with a certain officer in the company, drive the apparatus and operate the pumps at a fire. Jimmy Ferretti was my regular chauffeur and whenever I worked he usually drove the apparatus. He is about my age and grew up in the South Ozone Park section of Queens, not far from where I grew up in Howard Beach, and not far from the firehouse.

He lived in Seaford, Long Island. During the summer he enjoyed fishing on his boat and during the fall he went deer hunting. He had a reputation for never actually bagging a deer. Al Merk was Lieutenant Joe Mill's regular chauffeur. He is a big good-natured guy and often filled in as an aide in the battalion. He was a racing car enthusiast. Nick D'Onofrio was Lieutenant Cliff Payan's regular chauffeur. He had once run unsuccessfully for the position of Queens Trustee of the Uniformed Firefighters Association. John Ostrick was an experienced firefighter and was the junior man in the group with me. He is built like a bull and I found him to be totally reliable at a fire or emergency, or in the firehouse. Ralph Scerbo was not assigned to Engine 308, but was one of the regular aides in Battalion 51. He is a good-humored guy and a good aide. I had heard that he was an excellent baseball player.

I was anxious to get going. D'Onofrio and Scerbo were not ready yet, so it worked out that I, Ostrick, Ferretti, and Merk started out for Cunningham Park in Ostrick's car. D'Onofrio and Scerbo followed in another car. At this point none of us knew where we would be going beyond Cunningham Park, what we would be doing, or where we would end up. I was not sure that we would end up outside of New York City or even New York State before the night was over. As far as we all knew the attacks were still going on. I told the guys to bring money with them in case we had to buy food. Someone, I think it may have been Ostrick, said that he was sure that there would be food for us somewhere. I brought money anyhow. We tried to find something to bring with us that might help, but as I said, every spare tool was gone already. We ended up taking one large sealed water cooler bottle with us. Aside from our own personal gear, this was the only thing we brought.

Ostrick, since he was the youngest and the junior man, ended up carrying it.

Ostrick drove a well-worn Chevy S10 pickup with front and rear seats and an enclosed station-wagon type back. It was a ghetto car in the finest sense of the word. We all threw our gear in the back along with the water bottle. The rear seats looked a little cramped. Ferretti hopped in the back, and I offered to sit in the back since Merk is taller than me, allowing him the extra leg room in the front. He, however, insisted that I sit in the front, the traditional riding position for the officer on duty. Since this was, after all, a ghetto car, the back of the front passenger seat was loose, and I had to ride leaning forward so as not to keep banging into Merk's legs.

At some point we ended up eastbound on Union Turnpike, heading for Cunningham Park. The conversation in the car had its ups and downs. Everyone was pretty subdued. No one was venting any anger or showing any fear. I expressed some concern about what we would be confronted with down there. Ferretti mentioned how he originally thought that the plane strikes had been accidents and that some air traffic controller was going to be in real trouble. It sounds ridiculous now but it brings up the point that the reality of this thing took some time to sink in. No normal person could have imagined this horrible attack. Ostrick said that someone at the firehouse suggested we stop off and buy some throwaway cameras before going down there. I think he may have been seeking my approval, but I didn't say anything. It probably would have been a good idea but on the other hand I did not want to stop and waste time looking for cameras. At any rate we didn't stop.

As I said, the conversation went up and down. A group of New York City firefighters traditionally joke around, no matter how bad things are, and we did the same. However, after some light moments we immediately went back into the dark reality. We passed St. John's University on our right and then about a block further passed a bar-restaurant, The Sly Fox, which I had frequented on occasion about twenty years earlier. I made a joke about doing so, which got a laugh and broke the tension for a moment at least. We reached Cunningham Park and Ostrick pulled into the parking lot.

CUNNINGHAM PARK

We removed our gear from the back of the car and made our way to a makeshift command post set up near the entrance of the park. There were scores of firefighters and officers milling about already. The command post consisted of a table with some folding chairs. One or two firefighters or officers manned it. I reported in and was asked to fill out a small form called the BF-4, also known as the Riding List. An officer fills out one of these forms and a carbon copy at the beginning of every tour. He or she carries one in his or her shirt pocket (it is just that size), and clips the other to a holder on the dashboard of the apparatus. The form lists every member working the tour in that particular company, along with their group number, their assignment, and their riding position on the apparatus. I simply listed my name and the guys I had with me, and wrote "Day of Infamy" on the line for the date.[5]

John Ostrick was still lugging the large water bottle with him. We decided to leave it at the command post in the park. It was too cumbersome and those at the command post may have been able to use it there. D'Onofrio and

Scerbo showed up a short time after we arrived and they joined us. They had their gear and Scerbo brought a large athletic bag with him, which came in handy later. Buses were shuttling firefighters downtown so we waited for the next available one. There were firefighters and officers from our division already at the park. I recognized a number of guys with whom I had worked in the past. There were a few from our battalion and I asked one or two if they wanted to join up with our group. They declined since everyone seemed to have enough guys from their own companies. I said hello to Bobby Moscia. Bob was the Captain of Engine 294 on Jamaica Avenue, in Richmond Hill, also part of our battalion. We had grown up in the same Queens neighborhood of Howard Beach, but I never really knew him. I lived in old Howard Beach and he lived in the newer Rockwood Park section. We worked as firefighters in the same firehouse in the East New York section of Brooklyn in the mid to late 1980s. He was assigned to Ladder 175 and I was in Engine 332, both housed in the same quarters on Bradford Street. Bob, or "Moose" as he was known, was a classic firehouse instigator. He usually had a big grin on his face, talked loud, and had a wide-mouthed, booming, "in-your-face" laugh. When I said hello to him on this occasion he just walked by with a sort of disassociated look. He shook his head and repeated in a subdued voice, "Stupid people. Stupid people."

THE BUS RIDE

Finally two buses pulled up and we piled on. There were two battalion chiefs, a number of company officers (captains and lieutenants), and firefighters. Each battalion chief went into one of the two buses. Each bus filled and my thought was that when we got to the scene we would operate as a "battalion" with whichever chief was on our bus. The chief on our bus was a tall, slim guy whose name I can't remember. I did not know him nor could I remember ever working with him. The other chief worked in our battalion as a covering chief a number of times. He was a compact, talkative guy and I had many conversations with him in the kitchen of Engine 308 when he worked in the 51 Battalion. He was in the first bus and I and my guys were in the second. I delayed getting on the bus so the Engine 308 guys ended up sitting near the front as did the chief. I sat in one of the seats facing into the aisle. We piled our gear in the aisle which made for cramped conditions. The chief stood near the front. Our driver was a large black woman. The buses made their way to the Long Island Expressway and we took off for Manhattan.

Somewhere along the route the chief in our bus decided that he needed to speak with the chief in the first bus. He knew that the other chief had a cell phone but didn't know the number. He asked me to call Division 13, to which we were all assigned, to get the cell number or at least his home number. If we failed to get the cell number from the Division, he wanted me to call the other chief's home to get the number from his wife. I thought that this wasn't the best idea since it would only heighten the anxiety of the chief's wife if she had not heard from him. Anyway, I tried but we never did get him on the phone.

I got restless on the bus so I stood up and positioned myself in the well of the front door. I knelt on my left knee and stood on the lowest step with my right foot. I was right up against the front window and could speak to the driver.

We were barreling west on the Long Island Expressway when the driver started to make little grunting screams almost to herself. Finally I asked her what was wrong. She told me that there was a radio link between the two buses and she was trying to reach the other bus but could not.

The Expressway was completely empty except for emergency vehicles and our buses. Police officers guarded the entrance and exit ramps, allowing no unauthorized traffic. I think we pulled over once and the two chiefs conferred. We continued on to Manhattan, passing the Long Island City section of Queens on our right and the Greenpoint section of Brooklyn, where I had worked as a lieutenant, on our left.

I spoke to the driver and could not help kidding her a little. I complimented her on her driving and asked her if she would be interested in coming on the Fire Department and getting assigned to my company. I told her I would put her in group 14, which was my group, which meant that she would be driving me. This got a little laugh from my guys sitting up front since Jimmy Ferretti was my regular chauffeur in group 14.

There was some discussion about what route we should take into Manhattan. It was either go through the Queens-Midtown Tunnel which goes under the East River, or take the Queensborough Bridge (the 59th Street Bridge) which goes over. Most of the guys favored the bridge on the premise that if someone blew up the bridge, we would have at least a slim chance of survival. If someone blew up the tunnel, well, that would be it. It is important to remember that at this point we had no idea that the attacks were over. We fully expected to see more planes going into more buildings. It was just a question of where and when. We passed a computerized billboard on the left. It flashed the word "Peace." Right behind it was the terrible cloud from downtown. Everyone took a long look at the cloud and what could be seen of the skyline. I remarked that downtown looked like a mouth with a couple of teeth missing.

The decision was made to take the tunnel by the bus drivers alone. It was the easiest route, since the Long Island Expressway, which we were on, led directly to the tunnel. We would have had to maneuver through side streets to get to the bridge. Right before we went through I turned to the rest of the guys on the bus and made the Sign of the Cross. We went through without any problem and emerged in Manhattan just above 34th Street.

MANHATTAN

The Manhattan Streets were characteristically crowded with pedestrians. Many of the people had dazed or shocked looks on their faces. Although it was early afternoon, many of them were trying to find ways to evacuate the city and get home. The buses stopped once or twice and the chief and I got out. I believe he got out to speak to some police officer or to clear traffic. My biggest fear was that the buses would take off without me when I got out. We ended up heading south but I have no idea of the avenue. At one point we stopped and picked up two police officers. I don't remember where we let them off, but I do not think that they went all the way down with us.

In hindsight we know what happened that day. The attacks took place within a certain amount of time, the buildings collapsed at a certain time, and they fell in a certain way. At the time, however, we were not sure of anything. For all we knew the attacks were still going on. It would not have surprised any of us to see more planes coming in. Also, I had no idea that the towers had collapsed more or less straight down on themselves in a pancake fashion. When the Trade Center was bombed in 1993, the intent of the animals who did it was to have the tower hinge over and crash across Lower Manhattan. I had often wondered what it would have been like if that had happened. I was not sure that this hadn't happened now.

As we approached downtown I began to be concerned about my brother Michael. At the time he was a court clerk at 346 Broadway, a building I worked in when I was a Court Officer in the mid-1970s before I went on the Fire Department. This building is on Broadway between Worth and Leonard Streets about a half mile north of the Trade Center. The Trade Center towers were a quarter mile high.

We continued south through Manhattan on what I think was an east side avenue. Eventually we got on Broadway probably around Fourteenth Street. At all times the horrendous cloud from downtown loomed in front of us. Eventually we passed 346 Broadway and I saw with great relief that the building was unscathed. I took a quick look for Michael as we passed the building but did not spot him. It was around this time I began to notice the gray dust. It got thicker as we went south and after a few blocks it covered the streets and buildings like snow. Of course, none of us had ever seen anything like it.

DOWNTOWN

The buses pulled over to the right on Broadway just north of Chambers Street. We piled off with our gear and assembled on the sidewalk. I thanked and said good-bye to our driver before the bus pulled away and wished her luck. I felt that she was in as much danger as any of us. We were complete strangers but now we had a bond as New Yorkers in a crisis. That was the way it was with everyone we encountered from that point on.

I do not know where the chief on our bus was from or where he worked, but he seemed not to know what direction the Trade Center was from our point. This seemed a little strange because if anything was evident, it was the giant cloud of smoke to the south. He asked me which route we should take and I told him I knew. He also asked if we should don our bunker gear already. The gear consists of a heavy coat and an equally heavy pair of pants with thick pads in the knees. The pants are held up by suspenders. Short but heavy boots are attached to the pants by snaps so that when donning the gear one steps into the folded down pants directly into the boots and then pulls the pants up.[6]

With the weight of the gear in mind and since it was a fairly warm day, I told the chief that we should carry the gear until we got closer to the site. Most of us did, but everyone wore his helmet from that point on.[7]

I gave my guys a brief pep talk somewhere. It may have been back before boarding the bus in Cunningham Park, but I think it was on Broadway. I told them to stick together, keep me in sight, and stay with me. I told them I thought our chances of finding anyone alive were slim to none and it was important that none of us end up casualties too.

When we were ready I directed the group west on Chambers Street. We turned south at the next corner, Church Street, and headed straight for the roiling cloud of smoke. There were a number of feelings and impressions crowding in as we made our way down Church Street. One was a strange feeling of exhilaration. It was by no means happiness, just exhilaration. I had worked downtown years ago as a court officer, and I had been down there many times since. The streets and sidewalks were always choked with pedestrians and traffic. Now, with the exception of emergency personnel and vehicles, the streets were virtually empty. We walked right down the middle of Church Street. One had the feeling of "Well, the federal government failed to protect us, the politicians failed, the intelligence agencies failed, the military failed, now it was left to us to pick up the pieces and save whomever we could." It felt as if we owned the streets and we probably did.

Other impressions were from literary sources. I thought of a scene at the beginning of John Steinbeck's *The Grapes of Wrath* where he described the Dust Bowl in Oklahoma, and how a walking man raised a cloud of dust to his waist. That is how firefighters in front of us looked as they walked along. Dante's *Inferno* also came to mind. Conditions and damage got worse with every short block we walked.

Another feeling was that of a rising anxiety which I had to keep under control. We did not know with what we would be faced in a few short blocks. I thought that by the time we reached the Trade Center we literally would be wading through piles of bodies and body parts. I had to suppress that thought by imagining that I was physically pushing it down, because I was not sure that I would not lose it if that proved to be the case.

We passed countless civilian, fire, and police vehicles as we walked along. Many were damaged and all were covered with the dust. It looked as if a crew had already come though with pay-loader and piled some of the vehicles on top of one another or pushed them to the side to clear the street. It gave me a fleeting thought that we were too late and that all the important work was being done already. I tried to take note of the company numbers on the sides of fire apparatus, and determine if I knew any of the members assigned to those companies.

I also gave a thought to some of the new guys assigned to Engine 308. The Department was using what was called the "Rotation System" for probationary firefighters at the time. Under this system a brand new probationary firefighter (a proby) fresh out of the fire academy was assigned to a unit. He or she stayed with the unit for nine months to a year and then rotated to another company for a like period of time. The system called for two rotations before the probationary firefighter returned to his or her originally assigned unit. The purpose of this system was to familiarize a new firefighter with different parts of the city, different buildings, and different types of fire companies, i.e. engine and ladder companies. I also believe that it was designed to keep a new firefighter slightly off balance for a while and not let him or her get too comfortable too fast.

At the time I had four probies assigned to the company and they were all out on the first leg of their rotation. I also had four probies from other companies detailed to 308. I took stock and realized that one of my probies, Steve Cox, had been rotated to Ladder Company 10, right across Liberty Street from the south side of the World Trade Center. Steve is a big, tough, easy-going guy. He is a lacrosse player and a cooperative guy around the firehouse. I liked having him in the company. I hoped that he had not been working that day or the night before. I though sadly that if he had been I would never see him again.

We were just a block or two north of the Trade Center when we stopped to don our bunker gear. We took off our shoes and put them in the athletic bag that Ralph Scerbo had brought along. Somewhere and somehow the guys came into possession of a helmet belonging to a member of Ladder 146. That went into the athletic bag also. Ralph and John Ostrick carried the large bag between them.

The dust became heavier and the smoke more acrid as we approached the Trade Center. We had no respiratory protection. Part of our bunker gear consists of a nomex hood which you place over your head and around your neck like a heavy turtleneck until you need it. Since it was issued by the city as part of our protective gear, one is required to wear it on one's head at a fire. It protects the ears and neck from burns. Like the bunker gear it is also controversial. Most firefighters do not like it since it insulates them from their surroundings. I had my hood around my neck at this point and brought part of it up over my mouth as a mask through which to breathe. I could not take it though. I was not able to get enough air and it was starting to make me feel claustrophobic, so I lowered it again.

About a block or two north of the Trade Center, at Murray Street, one of my guys said "Look over there." I turned to my left and saw a crushed jet engine on the corner. The sight was so incongruous that I intentionally unfocused my eyes, afraid of what I might see next.

Right about this time we heard the cries of "Run! Run!" and a stampede of police and firefighters came at us from the direction of the Trade Center. Apparently they thought that Trade Center Building Seven, which was across Vesey Street just to the north of the main Trade Center complex, was about to collapse. We took a few tentative steps in the opposite direction and then the stampede petered out. The building did not collapse at this point. It would last a few more hours. Also around this time we were directed to go to a Fire Department command post to the east at the intersection of Broadway and Ann Street. Before we changed direction a number of police officers came out of the dust cloud to the west and handed us painters' dust masks. I took two, putting one over my mouth and nose, and the other in the pocket of my bunker coat. This was the only respiratory protection we would have.

BROADWAY AND ANN

The intersection of Broadway and Ann Street in Lower Manhattan is a busy and crowded intersection. Fulton Street and Park Row also come together here at the south end of City Hall Park. When we arrived we found the intersection crowded, not with pedestrians and traffic, but with firefighters. The command post consisted of some kind of table in the middle of the intersection, just off the southeast corner of Ann Street. I cannot describe it better than that since I never really got too close to it to have a good look. The chief in command of large Fire Department operations sets up a command post, usually at second alarms or up. His aide opens a metallic table on which a rough diagram of the building can be drawn. Magnetic markers with the numbers of different fire companies are placed on the board to mark where the companies are operating. It is traditionally referred to as the "Monopoly board." I'm not sure if the chief in command had one here.

Companies that do not respond on an initial alarm or do not get put to work right away report in to the command post for assignment. Rather, the company officer reports in to the command post. The firefighters stand fast at a staging area nearby and remain there until their officer receives an assignment. I went to the command post and my guys went to the staging area, in this case in front of the Woolworth Building about a half block north on Broadway.

I joined the line with a bunch of other fire officers. Everyone was so eager to be put to work that we practically stood on top of one another. My friend, Mike Blakely, from the Western Writers of America, has a song entitled "It's About to get Western," in which he describes cowboys "Riding brim to brim from the ranch to the rodeo." That is what it was like. My helmet's front brim was almost touching the back of the officer's helmet in front of me, and the same for the officer behind me.

The officer in command of the post was Deputy Chief Haring. I never worked with him but I remember that at one time he was in charge of Hazardous Material training, and I had attended classes he taught.[8] Chief Haring obviously was very busy. I believe he had a battalion chief and one or two firefighters helping him. I was not close enough to see what he was doing or hear what he was saying. The line did not move and no one seemed to be getting assigned to do anything except for chiefs. The two battalion chiefs we had traveled with went to the command post and were quickly given assignments. That was the last we saw of them, and so much for my belief about operating as battalions under their command.

Things were a bit chaotic. Much of the top echelon of the Fire Department was killed when the towers collapsed. A command post had been set up initially in Tower One, the first to be hit. Later the overall command post moved to the driveway/loading bay of the World Financial Center right across West Street from the Trade Center. When the buildings fell, this post was wiped out. If any survived it was only because Chief of Department Peter Ganci directed members to go north after the first collapse.

The command fell to three or four independent posts located around the four sides of the sixteen acres of the World Trade Center complex. The Department radio system (radios in the fire apparatus which communicate with the dispatcher system), and the handi-talkies (radios that firefighters carry on their persons) were over-taxed by this time. Much communication between the individual posts was carried on by runners.

What followed was hours of frustration and waiting. None of the officers on line strayed from the line and there was a minimum of conversation. Everyone's attention was riveted on the command post for fear that they would miss their chance to be assigned.

RANDOM OBSERVATIONS

The time...

Tower One, the first to be hit but the second to collapse, fell at 10:29 in the morning. I believe that we arrived downtown within one and one-half hours after this, but I have no verification of the time. It was early afternoon.

The conditions...

The command post stood one short block from the northeast corner of the World Trade Center complex. Saint Paul's Chapel occupies one small block and stood between us and the Trade Center property. World Trade Center Building Five burned out of control just on the other side and across Church Street from Saint Paul's Chapel. A good portion of Building Five was still standing. The yellowish-gray dust flew through the air like a blizzard and covered everything. The dust was from 425,000 cubic yards of concrete in the Trade Center, in addition to millions of square feet of sheet-rock that made up the office walls, and all the glass in the buildings. Much of this material instantly pulverized when the buildings fell. There was probably a good bit of asbestos mixed in. Whatever it was made of, it was very irritating to the eyes and throat. It was not so thick that one could not look up and see the crystal clear blue sky above. At one point I looked down at the dust under my boots and thought that just a short time ago I had my bare feet in the clean white sand at Jones Beach.

Along with the dust flying through the air there was paper—forms, letters, pages of books, and scraps—like some weird ticker-tape parade. They sailed all over the place caught on the winds of the narrow streets of Lower Manhattan. I was tempted to pick up some pages and read them but I could not bring myself to. It seemed like some kind of invasion of privacy. It struck me that just a few hours ago these papers all carried some importance; transmitting and recording information on lives, businesses, finance, health, etc. Now they were meaningless. I looked down and right near the toe of my boot was a blank check torn neatly in two, with the two halves lying right beside one another along the tear.

The place...

The location of the command post was surrounded by New York City history. Just west and across Broadway was Saint Paul's Chapel where George Washington worshipped while in New York. One half block north on Broadway was the Woolworth Building, which had been the tallest building in the city from 1913 until 1937, when the Empire State Building was built. A bit further north, City Hall stood beyond City Hall Park. Looking east from there was Park Lane South and the Manhattan footing of the Brooklyn Bridge. The office building right behind us to the east was built on the sight of one of P.T. Barnum's famous museums. The studio of Civil War photographer Mathew Brady once stood across the street to the south of Saint Paul's. A few blocks further south along Broadway is Trinity Church. Alexander Hamilton is buried in its churchyard. Now his grave, as the ones in the churchyard of Saint Paul's, was covered with the dust and papers of the Trade Center. I wondered what Hamilton and Washington would have felt, knowing what had been done to their people.

Sights and sounds...

There was a general buzz from the command post, but it was impossible to hear what was being said. Someone at the command post decided that the lines of officers waiting should be more orderly, since we were all naturally crowding toward the table. Deputy Chief Haring and a battalion chief assisting him announced that they wanted three separate lines. They wanted engine officers who were there with companies (four or five firefighters) on the left, ladder company officers with enough personnel to operate as a company in the middle, and officers who were there on their own without any members of their companies on the right. In addition to sorting this out the chiefs kept waving everyone back from the tables. Of course, this only caused more confusion. I lined up on the left as the chief indicated. Since he was facing us, his left was on the opposite side.

One captain, with whom I had worked when we were lieutenants in the 11th Division but whose name escaped me, walked around in a total fog. It was actually funny. The battalion chief finally came down the line trying to straighten things out and he was even laughing. I quipped, "Hey chief, some of these ladder company guys are having trouble with the concept of 'right and left.'" He and a few others laughed. It was typical firehouse engine/ladder company rivalry humor. It wasn't that funny but it was a tension reliever. There were other attempts at humor despite the circumstances. It was as if we had to reassure ourselves of who we were and help bolster one another.

Every now and then a hollow metallic explosion went off from the direction of the Trade Center. They probably were car and truck tires exploding from the fires. Another distinct sound heard once or twice was that of jet planes. We would look up at the sound of a jet (I never did see any of them), exchange a glance with someone else, and then look to the right and left to see in what direction it would be best to run when the time came. However, in a few seconds someone said, "F-15," and everyone relaxed a bit. It was just like in the war movies—"It's one of ours."

Myself...

I still wore my bunker pants, helmet, and dust mask. Even though it was fairly warm I probably wore the heavy bunker coat if for no other reason then to keep the dust off of me. The dust and smoke from the fires became extremely irritating. There was nothing any of us could do about it other than duck into a building for some relief, but no one was going to leave the line to do that. Our helmets have eye shields that stand straight out from the brim. They are on springs and can just be flipped down when needed.

They are never used at fires since the face piece of the Scott air pack protects the eyes. The only time anyone uses the eye shield is when they are cutting something with the portable power saw or with a torch. Most of the eye shields are so scratched and dirty that they are difficult to see through anyway. I put mine down. They did not seal off my eyes and the dust still swirled around them, but I thought that they would at least keep something from blowing directly into my eyes. A Fire Department pickup truck pulled up to the intersection and unloaded boxes of power saws. Sometimes these saws come with plastic goggles. I asked the driver if there were any, hoping to grab a pair, but he said there were none.

At some point after we arrived downtown I became aware of a raging thirst. I hadn't had any water since I was at the beach that morning. Someone handed me a plastic bottle of water. I don't remember who or where, but I had it with me while on line at the command post. I took some sips and offered the bottle to a few others standing near me but they declined. I unbuttoned my shirt and put the bottle inside since there was no room in the pockets of my bunker coat. That became my canteen for the rest of the day.

Standing in one place or position for a long time usually bothers my back. I had surgery on a herniated disk a few years earlier, which cleared up the problem, but my back still bothers me if I stand too long. I did not experience any problem with my back at this time.

Friends…

I saw a number of people with whom I had worked in the past while standing in line. I also saw people with whom I had grown up and gone to school at various times in my life. I had the impression that different parts of my life were playing out in front of me. It was similar to the feeling I had at Jones Beach hours earlier.

I saw Joe Hands there. Joe is a compact guy with a gravelly, nasal voice. He came on the job maybe two years after I did and we were firefighters together in Engine 332 in the East New York section of Brooklyn years before. At the present time he also was a Captain in the 13th Division as I was, but I don't believe he had his own company.

Normally if I saw Joe I would go over and talk to him but I wasn't about to get off the line to do so now. Whenever I see him we invariably end up talking about a cellar fire we had in East New York one freezing night about twenty years earlier, and always have a laugh about it. We were working that night with Captain Higgins of Engine 227, but who was on overtime in 332. Capt. Higgins was a tough fire officer. I had the nozzle and Joe had backup that tour. We caught the fire late at night or in the wee-morning hours, and things went haywire rapidly.[9]

Capt. Higgins had four sons who were firefighters or fire officers at the time. What I did not know was that at that moment one of them, Lieutenant Timothy Higgins, was one block away under the rubble of the World Trade Center.

John Garvin was there. John and I were lieutenants in the same firehouse on Greenpoint Avenue in Brooklyn a few years before. I was assigned to Engine 238 and he was in Ladder 106. He had gotten promoted to captain a short time after I had and, after going through the Captains Management Development Program, had been assigned back to Ladder 106 as captain. This rarely happens in the FDNY, but as will be seen, it happened to lieutenants from both companies in this firehouse. I tried to catch John's eye to say hello at least, but he kept his face toward the command post and seemed not to blink an eye.

Captain Tom Robson walked around the command post area. I never worked with him but I knew him from the Bureau of Training, where he was the executive officer. For a time I worked at the Bureau of Training while working on the Department's magazine *WNYF (With New York Firefighters)*. Tom has the unique distinction of being a fire officer *and* a practicing dentist. I believe he has since been promoted to Battalion Chief. I did not speak to him there.

I also saw Jerry Migliore. Jerry had been a firefighter in Engine 236 when I had been in Engine 332 in East New York. Both firehouses were single engine companies and both were located on Liberty Avenue, about twelve blocks apart.[10] Later we were both lieutenants in the 11th Division in Brooklyn. I was in Engine 238 and Jerry was "bouncing" (not assigned to a specific company but filling in wherever needed on any particular tour). At the time I believe he was still a lieutenant and had been assigned to a Brooklyn engine company. I do not remember the company but I know that they lost a guy or guys at the Trade Center. Jerry has since been promoted to captain and then battalion chief. Besides being a good guy, Jerry is also a CPA and my accountant. I do not remember speaking to him at the command post.

Activity…

There was a good deal of activity around us as we waited for assignment. A number of people stood behind us on the corner, some were probably civilians. All looked as if they wanted to help somehow. There was a small group of young black guys wearing Fire Department dress shirts and ties. They may have been EMTs, or may have been part of the department's recruitment unit, or may have been in the Fire Department cadet program. They seemed a bit lost, wanting to do something but not sure what they could do. They had no protective gear.

A steady stream of police officers and other officials passed behind us on their way south on Broadway. A whole troop of Uniformed Court Officers passed by, all in light blue nylon jackets with "Court Officer" on the back. Court officers are peace officers who guard the New York State Criminal, Family, Civil, and Supreme Court houses. I was a court officer in criminal court from 1974 to 1977, before I went to the Fire Department. The court officers of today seem much more organized and professional than they did when I was one. I wanted to grab one and ask if anyone had seen my brother but I did not want to risk leaving the line to do so. Finally, another group of court officers came by and I spoke to one. She was a short, blond girl who had a stricken look on her face. I asked her if she knew Michael. She did and either said that she did not know where he was or that she had not seen him that day. I removed the dust mask and told her, "I'm his brother. If you see him, tell him that I'm here and that I'm okay." She said that she would and then went off south with the rest of the officers. I hoped that if I could make some contact with him, he could get word back to Kelly and/or my mother that I was all right. Also, if I found him and he was willing, I would put him to work with me. A little while later a bunch of court officers came back past us from the south. The girl to whom I had spoken came up to me again and assured me that she would tell Michael if she saw him. She seemed to be on the verge of crying.

Ferretti and then Scerbo came up to the line while I waited. I did not recognize them until they were right before me. This was due to the dust masks we all wore. They looked at my helmet to identify me, and I did not know them until I saw their helmets. They wanted to know if any progress was being made in getting us something to do. I could only tell them that no progress was being made and told them to stick together. They told me that they would be in front of the Woolworth Building.

At one point I saw guys carrying handfuls of new tools, like shovels and crowbars, etc. Someone said that firefighters broke into a closed hardware store and took every tool that could be used. I never found out if this was true or not.

Rumors and Stories…

We were still in the dark about what was going on in the rest of the city, the country, and whole world in general at this point. The FDNY is a rumor mill of monumental proportions under the best circumstances, so rumors began flying on the lines at the command post. The things said did not have any uncertainty about them. All were stated as fact carved in stone. One story told of how police shot and killed a man on the Brooklyn Bridge who was carrying a package and refused to stop. This proved to be false. Another one was that police stopped a van or truck on the George Washington Bridge and the truck had been carrying explosives—also untrue. We heard in no uncertain terms that the Capitol Building and the Washington Monument in Washington D.C. had been hit by planes. We did not even know about the Pentagon or the plane in Pennsylvania at this point. Someone stated that the United States was already bombing Afghanistan.

Hearing about the Capitol and the Washington Monument confirmed to me that all of this was still going on and that we were in the middle of it. A wave of sadness washed over me as I thought of the beautiful structures destroyed by these animals. I thought that they were not just out to murder us but were also going after our symbols as a people. I stood there looking north toward City Hall and did a quick inventory of some of my favorite places around the country. I hoped that officials closed the Golden Gate Bridge. I also said to myself, "I hope someone had the presence of mind to evacuate the Alamo." Then I thought, "Texans evacuating the Alamo? I don't think so!" It was a silly thought but it kind of gave me strength and perked me up a little.

Besides rumors, fire stories were related. One engine company lieutenant responded with his company on their apparatus. He told of how they were confronted with a block in which every car and truck on the street was on fire. Vehicle fires are extremely smoky and the smoke is extremely acrid. They started down the block, extinguishing one after the other. I don't remember if he said that they used one or two hose lines, but I do remember him saying that they were aided on their line or lines by police officers and civilians. The police officers and civilians would not have had any breathing protection from the acrid smoke. This story gave me a good feeling. I never felt prouder of New Yorkers or of being a New Yorker than at that moment. The city sometimes has a bad reputation with the rest of the country. However, when the chips are down, New Yorkers come together.

At one point I remember stepping off a curb on Broadway and I either stumbled, or I bent down to pick something up that I may have dropped. Immediately I felt two hands on my shoulders. I turned to my left and to see a young black gentleman holding me up. "Are you okay?" he asked. I said I was, and he shoved me forward as if to say, "All right, then get back in there and fight!" He disappeared into the dust as suddenly as he appeared.

But, back to the lieutenant's story, it stuck in my mind because of bad things too. He mentioned that the block on which they extinguished the fires was littered with human arms and legs.

Names…

Inevitably some conversation at the command post turned to those dead or missing and some very prominent names were mentioned. One was First Deputy Commissioner William Feehan. Bill Feehan had over forty years on the job, having served in every firefighting rank in addition to that of Fire Commissioner for a time. At the present he was second in command to Fire Commissioner Thomas Von Essen. Many felt that Feehan ran the fire fighting side of the job. He was a tough but friendly official, whose whole life was the Fire Department. His wife passed away a few years earlier and he lived alone in the Rockaway section of Queens. It had been mentioned humorously in headquarters that he was getting a bit absent-minded and his utilities at home were being turned off now and then because he forgot to pay the bills. My father, William F. Groneman Jr., had been a fireman for 27 years and a ladder company chauffeur assigned to Ladder Company 6 in Chinatown. Feehan had been a lieutenant there and they worked in the same groups. He always liked to tell the story of how upset and nervous my father became one time when Feehan had to assign him as acting lieutenant for part of a tour. He shared that story with my mother and my family when I had received an administrative award the previous April.

My mother's name is Jean. Commissioner Feehan always called her "Jeanie."

Another name was that of Chief of Department Peter Ganci. He was the highest ranking uniformed member of the FDNY, and in firefighting there is probably no more prestigious position. Chief Ganci was a friendly guy and a tough firefighter. He never identified himself to strangers as "The Chief of Department," but simply as "a firefighter." He was a former paratrooper and had a chest full of Fire Department medals and citations. I remember Chief Ganci from my first tour as a lieutenant. I had spent most of my firefighting career in Engine 332 in East New York, but worked my first tour as lieutenant in Ladder 106 in Greenpoint. I had very little ladder company experience, having only worked in the very slow Ladder 173 in Howard Beach (my home neighborhood) for six months before getting promoted. Also, there was no training for the position of lieutenant, so one day I was a firefighter and the next day an officer. I went on my first run with Ladder 106 on a night tour. Chief Ganci was the Battalion Chief who responded on the box. He obviously saw that I was brand new. He asked me where I had worked before getting promoted. I told him I had worked six months in Ladder 173, but then quickly added, "But I worked ten years in Engine 332." He said, "Well, forget everything from 173 and remember everything from 332 and you'll do okay."[11]

Another name I heard was that of Assistant Chief Donald Burns. At the time he was one of the City-Wide Tour Commanders. These were high-ranking chiefs, one of whom worked every tour and handled the biggest jobs throughout the city. Chief Burns was a very knowledgeable fire officer, as are all the chiefs who achieve this rank and position. He served as Chief of Operations at one time. I was promoted to captain in January, 1996, and assigned to work as his assistant in headquarters, while he was Chief of Operations, as part of my learning experience in the Captain's Management Development Program. He was a tall guy, at least 6'4". He always seemed to have a little grin on his face and he had a funny high-pitched, cackling laugh.

Assistant Chief Gerard Barbara was mentioned. He worked out of headquarters at the time and I think he was the Chief of Fire Prevention. He was a very nice individual—a gentleman in Fire Department parlance. I had only spoken to him once or twice. He had recently called me into his office at headquarters because he had attended a conference in San Antonio, Texas. He had heard about my interest in the Alamo and Texas and we chatted for a while. I wish I had known him better.

I heard the name of Battalion Chief Ray Downey. Chief Downey was one of the most renowned firefighters in the country. Within the FDNY he was known as "God." He was a nationally-known expert on rescue operations and he had published books on the subject. He also wrote a number of articles for our magazine, *WNYF*. He was a former U.S. Marine, tough, aggressive, and fearless. At the time he was the officer in charge of the Special Operations Command (SOC). This consisted of all the specialized units in the Department, such as the five Rescue companies, the Squad companies, the Hazardous Material Unit, the Marine companies, and a few others. He was one of the FDNY members who went to help during the Oklahoma City bombing. I remembered him as a lieutenant instructor in the FDNY training academy when I first came on the job. I and other probies were in a smoke-filled stairwell in one of the training buildings, choking our lungs out. Lt. Downey looked down on us from above, where the smoke was thicker, without coughing a bit and with a look of utter scorn on his face. A sense of unreality started to come over me when I heard his name. He had been considered indestructible.

A profound sadness accompanied the mention of Captain Terry Hatton of Rescue Company 1. I had been promoted to captain with Terry. He was a straight shooter and a very competent and highly-regarded firefighter. It was said that there was no one better on the fire floor, one of the highest compliments a New York City Firefighter can receive. His father was a retired chief. Terry was tall, about 6'5", and he had the face of a leprechaun. He laughed with a deep chuckle when something struck him funny. I did not know him very well but I liked him.

We went through the Captains' Management Program for newly promoted captains, and were halfway through when all of us met with Commissioner Von Essen in order to be reassigned to new management projects. Terry had just asked me about the books I write and was interested. Von Essen asked at the meeting if anyone would be interested in trying to get *WNYF* magazine back into publication after about a year or two hiatus. Terry enthusiastically encouraged me to do this. I took on the assignment and the magazine was back in publication within a few months.

I could go on about Terry. He had married Beth Patrone, an assistant to Mayor Rudolph Giuliani, a few years earlier. It was a real New York City romance story. Neither of them knew it on September 11, but they were expecting a child.

The last time I saw Terry was just about a year earlier. We had just taken the Battalion Chief's exam and were standing on a street corner in Manhattan having an enjoyable conversation. He stood in the street and I stood on the curb and I still had to look up at him.

Someone mentioned that the Department's Catholic Chaplain, Father Mychal Judge had been killed, and that his body had been carried into Saint Peter's Catholic Church just a block north of the Trade Center and placed at the altar. I did not know Father Judge but I probably had seen him at any number of Department functions. There is an often reproduced photo of him being carried on a chair by a number of firefighters, a police lieutenant, and civilians.

The most surprising name I heard was that of Fire Commissioner Von Essen. He was a controversial commissioner since he had been the head of the Uniformed Firefighters' Association before being appointed commissioner by Mayor Giuliani. In other words he went from representing the laborers (firefighters) to being their top manager. Many firefighters felt betrayed by this. He was also resented by some for bringing the Emergency Medical Service system into the Department. This necessitated engine companies responding on every EMS run. Von Essen tended to be tough and pugnacious. I worked with his brother Rod (Gerard) in Engine 332 years before. Rod was a bit of a character and earned a number of colorful firehouse nicknames. I had no problem with Von Essen although I knew he was not the most popular of Fire Commissioners. When his name was mentioned as having been killed, an officer on line said something like, "Good, he deserved it." Whatever one's feelings about Von Essen, this was way out of line. I gave the officer a disapproving look but didn't say anything. It was not the time for this kind of remark, nor to start fighting about it.

No one expressed any emotions when any of these names were mentioned. No one cried or expressed anger or outrage. No one went to pieces. Everyone just kept a deadpan face and absorbed the information. It just was not the time or place to feel or vent any emotions. We believed it was still going on and we were in it. Who knew what names would be added to the list, including our own before the day was over.

I believed everything I heard about the casualties, including that of Von Essen. I believed it right until the time he walked up to the command post. That was one rumor proven false. It gave hope that some of the others mentioned may have cheated death and made it. Von Essen conferred with Chief Haring for a while. I only caught a glimpse of his head and shoulders. I remember that he was in a shirt but had no jacket on. He was not there long and I don't know what they talked about. Where he went next I do not know.

One funny thing happened at the command post. Nerves started wearing thin as the afternoon wore on and guys started pushing forward toward the command post. After a while one of the chiefs announced that he needed two engine officers who had companies with them. Before most of us could answer two officers pushed their way forward ahead of many others and announced that they had companies with them. One of them was my friend Jerry Migliore. Obviously they thought that they were about to go right into action. The chief ordered them to get their guys and see how much bottled water they could find to bring back to the command post. Jerry's and the other officer's faces dropped. Boy, was I happy! I later told Jerry that it served him right for pushing ahead.

Good news, bad news...

At one point while still on line I heard, "Hey Cap!" I looked up to see Steve Cox, the proby I had been worried about, coming out of the dust toward me. I shook hands with him and told him I was glad to see him alive. That is the way it was. You were actually telling people that you were glad to see them alive. He had been in a cab on the West Side Highway coming into work at Engine 10 and Ladder 10. One or both planes already had hit while he was on his way and his cab was stuck in traffic. When Steve finally realized what was going on, he jumped out of the cab and ran down West Street toward the Trade Center and the Ten House. The first tower collapsed while he was running and he was caught in the rain of rubble and dust just a few blocks north. He finally made his way east and south to another firehouse. He had firefighting gear on when I saw him, and I don't know if it was his own or if he got it from another firehouse. I asked him if he wanted to join up with us but he declined. That was understandable because he had been working in 10 and 10 for about nine months. A number of their guys were missing and he wanted to work with others from the house on the search. It should be noted that I had to be reminded of this encounter by Steve himself some days or weeks after September 11. We were in 308's kitchen and I asked him what had happened to him that day. He asked me if I did not remember meeting him. It was only then that I was able to recall our brief encounter. That is how confusing things were.

Another encounter I had was not a happy one. A firefighter from Engine 202 came up to me and said, "Cap?" Engine 202 is housed with Ladder 101 in the Red Hook section of Brooklyn, very near the entrance of the

Brooklyn Battery Tunnel that connects Brooklyn to Lower Manhattan. When I was a lieutenant in Engine 238 in Greenpoint I worked overtime a few times in Engine 202 and Ladder 101, but I really did not know any of the guys there or remember them. I knew the firefighter was from Engine 202 by his helmet. I noticed that he was looking from my helmet to my eyes. Anyway, I responded to him and all he said was, "McShane is missing." It was only then I remembered that another one of my probies, Terence McShane, was on his rotation detail to Ladder 101.

McShane was new to the Fire Department but he was not new to New York City civil service. He had been a member of the Police Department for thirteen years before coming on to the Fire Department. He had even achieved the rank of sergeant in the NYPD, but he wanted to be a firefighter so badly that he took the demotion. He was married and his wife, Cathy, was a police officer too. They had three boys, one about seven and four-year-old twins. His father-in-law was a retired Fire Department captain.

Terry also had been a life guard on Long Island. He met Cathy at Overlook Beach, some miles east of Jones Beach. He was not big but slim and tough—toughened by playing rugby with his older brothers. He liked to talk a good deal in the firehouse, and he always had a story to tell—the Irish "gift of gab."

The guy from Engine 202 knew that Terry was from Engine 308 and he recognized that I was the captain of the company. I had not yet come to the realization that many Brooklyn companies responded to the Trade Center, and that many were caught in the collapse. I don't remember the rest of our conversation, but I hung my head as I tend to do when hearing bad or sad news that I am helpless to do anything about. I said. "All right, let me know if you get any other information." The stark reality of the day was beginning to set in.

TAKING COVER

The afternoon wore on with no assignments given out. Finally someone at the command post issued the order that everyone take cover in the office building directly to our left, at the corner of Broadway and Ann. The order was given in fear that World Trade Center Building Seven was about to collapse. This building was forty-seven stories tall and concerns about its stability caused the minor stampede on Church Street hours earlier. The lines broke up in frustration and I walked over to the Woolworth Building to collect my guys. A small tornado of dust and papers still spun in front of the famous skyscraper. I rounded up Engine 308's members and we walked back to the office building.

The lobby of this building was already crowded with firefighters by the time we entered. There was a security desk at the end of a long lobby and some turnstiles to the right of the desk. The air in the lobby was absolutely miserable. Every time the revolving doors turned, and they did often, another cloud of acrid smoke and dust billowed into the confined space. A young guard sat at the security desk where he and a group of firefighters watched news reports of the attack. The reports kept repeating footage of the second plane slamming into Tower 2. It was difficult to believe that what they watched on the TV happened only hours earlier and at less than a five-minute walk from where we stood.

I took my guys through the turnstiles. There was an elevator bank to the right and a hallway to the left. The air in this area was just as foul as the lobby. I walked down the hallway to the left in search of a restroom. Instead I found a loading dock with the doors to the outside closed and a group of firefighters using the drain in the middle of the loading dock floor for their restroom purposes. After a short search I found a restroom off of the loading dock.

I returned to the area of the elevators and ran into a group of firefighters from Engine 238 and Ladder 106 in Greenpoint, where I had been a lieutenant. I saw John Dean from 238 and Kenny Bohan from 106, and a few others. They sat on the floor leaning against the wall in the vicinity of the security desk. I said hello and shook hands with them. They told me that they had spoken to my brother Michael. He asked them if they knew me and it just so happened that he picked out a bunch of guys with whom I had worked. They were a little unclear about when and where they saw him, but I got the impression it was not that long ago and probably right out in the vicinity of the command post or staging area. At least I knew that he was all right and out there somewhere.

They also told me that almost the whole working crew Engine 238 that morning was missing. They had responded to the Trade Center from Greenpoint, as they had in 1993 when the Trade Center was bombed. At that time they had walked up to about the forty-eighth floor to help people. They also told me that Bill Romaka from 238, who had not been on duty but had come in later, found 238's chauffeur, Stanley Trojanowski, wandering the streets, almost incoherent after the collapses, trying to locate the rest of the company.[12]

I saw Dennis Wirbickas of 238 who had been my regular chauffeur when I worked there. He also lived in the same village of Malverne, Long Island, where I lived. Dennis is a bit of a character. When I saw him I immediately smiled, shook his hand and said, "Hey-ey," and he did the same. We forgot where we were for a second there, but immediately reigned it in.

At one point I walked back out in the main lobby and found Chris McKnight there. Chris and I had been lieutenants in 238 at the same time. We both were promoted to captain on the same day in January, 1996, along with another lieutenant, Kevin Malone, from the same house, but in Ladder 106. After the Captain's Management Program, Chris went back to 238 as the captain, just as John Garvin had with Ladder 106. Chris is a tall, slim guy and a marathon runner. I spoke to him for a while. One of the things he said was, "You know I think I may have lost my whole company," meaning the guys who were on duty that morning.

Someone passed through the crowd with a box of sport bars, which have the taste and consistency of asphalt. I took one because I was getting so hungry that I would have eaten asphalt. I returned to my guys at the elevator and we decided to have a look upstairs, where we found the air to be a little better. We also found a large, open office and we went in. Dennis Wirbickas and a few others drifted up also and followed us. I sat at one of the desks and found that the phones were working. Here was an opportunity for us to call home.

I know I tried to call home but I cannot actually remember getting through. The phone probably was busy. Kelly was receiving calls from all over the country by this time from friends wanting to know if I was all right. I found out later that the first to call was Jim Crutchfield of Tennessee, a good friend from the Western Writers of America.

I managed to get in touch with my mother in Howard Beach and told her to try to get in touch with Kelly to let her know that I was okay. I told her about the casualties and recited the names I had heard, starting with Bill Feehan. She expressed her shock when she heard that he was one of those killed. She told me that she heard from Michael. He had made his way uptown with a group of others, where they found an open bar. The proprietor invited people in and gave them free food and beer. I said to myself, "Ain't this a bitch! The world is coming to an end, and he falls head first into free beer!"

There was a container of towelettes on the desk. I cleaned my hands with some and considered cleaning my eyes with them. I thought better of that, however, since they contained alcohol and that would have made them worse. I briefly considered chewing one but luckily gave up on that idea. It would not have been the same in light of Michael's free beer.

I went back downstairs after making my calls, walked back into the lobby, and ran into Captain Mike DeGennaro. We had been firefighters in Engine 332 together until he "went across the floor," FDNY parlance for transferring to the other company, in this case, Ladder 175 in the same quarters. Mike is a solidly built guy with a wry sense of humor. He is also introspective. A number of times after firefighters' funerals we would get into a conversation about how it never ends. He would remark that no matter how many funerals there have been, there is always going to be another, and that someone out there is a "marked man." We did not go there on this occasion. It would have been too overwhelming. We did speak about the dust. It was he who stated that it was made up of all the sheetrock that separated the different offices and rooms of the Trade Center. I tried another sports bar at this point but didn't finish it. It was too revolting.

Soon someone from the command post came in and announced that this building was being evacuated, and that everyone should go across Broadway and into the Woolworth Building. No reason was given, but it had to do with the imminent collapse of Building Seven. I walked back upstairs where my guys and a number of other firefighters were. I announced the building was being evacuated and directed everyone to the Woolworth Building. We trudged across Broadway and north a half-block. The tornado of dust and papers still swirled.

We went in the front doors on Broadway and into the ornate marble lobby. There is a security desk in the middle where the lobby branches off to the right and left. Elevators are to the right, a small convenience store/coffee shop to the left, and a large staircase at the rear.

The lobby was filling up fast. I believe some portable lights run by generators had been set up. Since conditions in the other building were better on the second floor, I and my guys immediately went to the staircase and up. We turned right off the stairs to another small lobby with a few benches. We picked a spot directly to the right of the stairs and settled on the floor. There was a window there where one could look down on the main lobby.

I removed my gear including the bunker pants, and did not even bother to put my shoes on. The first thing I did was look for a restroom. I don't believe there was electricity in the building so I probably used a small flashlight. I don't remember it being particularly dark though. I turned right from where we had settled and went down a hallway with offices. As I walked along I suddenly felt dizzy and I staggered a little. I thought to myself that the smoke and fumes outside, plus the lack of any real food, had gotten to me. Then I heard Ralph Scerbo who was behind me say, "Hey, why did the whole building just move like that?" I found a small restroom which was quiet, clean and empty. I leaned my head against the mirror after washing out my eyes and had the feeling that I just wanted to stay in there.

I returned to the hallway, however, and heard guys talking about how Building Seven had just collapsed. Building Seven was just a half-block west of us, which is why the whole building moved. This is recorded as happening at 5:20 p.m., so this became one of the very few instances where I can link a time to what I was doing. Nine hours before I was getting out of the car in Parking Field 6 at Jones Beach.

A few guys had gone into offices. I went in one to take a look out of one of the windows. The window shade was a light gray color. I lifted the shade and everything outside was the same light gray color. I could not see a thing. Another giant dust cloud erupted through the streets when Building Seven collapsed. I found out later that some of the other guys from 308, who had gone to the site before my group, were on the west side at this time and ran to escape the cloud. One of our other probies, Steve Kelly, who at the time was detailed to another company ran and just made the corner of the Woolworth Building as the dust cloud swept by.

BROTHER MICHAEL

I later found out that my brother made his way back downtown, awash in free beer, and was in the vicinity of the Brooklyn Bridge by this time. He said that he heard a warning siren and saw people yelling and running. He did not know if another plane was coming in or if a building was collapsing. He ran for a three-foot-high wall on one of the approaches to the bridge, intending to jump over it. He looked over the wall and saw that it was about a six-to-eight-foot drop on the other side. He and a friend who was with him took the plunge and took cover.

At this point I should add something that Michael experienced that day. He had been sitting in his office that morning at 346 Broadway which, as I stated earlier, was about one-half mile north of the World Trade Center. He heard a loud metallic "boom" at about 8:46 a.m. and thought it was a large dumpster being dropped off the back of a truck. Someone ran into his office a short time later and said that a plane had hit the Trade Center. He and a group of people took the elevator and the stairs to the roof of his building which, at about thirteen stories, provided a clear view of the Trade Center towers. As soon as they got on the roof and looked south, the second plane which had been obscured from their view, came through Tower Two, causing a tremendous fireball. Michael said that the heat of this fireball drove them back on the roof, despite being one-half mile away. The Federal Building stood on Broadway just a block south of his building and loomed above it. Michael immediately knew what was going on and that the Federal Building could very well be the next target. He immediately got everyone off the roof and began an evacuation of his building. Later he was out on Broadway when one of the Towers collapsed. He said that the people running up Broadway looked like those in one of the monster movies from the 1950s. He related most of this information the following night on the phone. He also described in a shaky, emotionally charged voice how he saw many people tumble out of the tower when the second plane came through.

MEANWHILE

Back in the Woolworth Building we were shooed out of the office by a young, nervous security guard. I returned to our spot in the second floor lobby and lay down on the floor, using my bunker gear as a pillow. The other guys from 308 sat around, as did clusters of guys from different fire companies. Everyone mostly kept to their own group. One of our group remarked about being hungry and John Ostrick offered to go down to the first floor to see if he could get anything from the coffee shop. He returned with one or two boxes filled with candy, sports bars, warm drinks, etc. I do not know if the shop was opened and the owners gave the stuff away or if our guys broke in and appropriated the food. Either way, I thank the owners. It did not matter anyway since many of us still had the attitude that it was the end of the world and we were all dead already. We all nosed through the supplies. Hunger may have nudged me to try another sports bar. I was very thirsty so I took a plastic bottle of warm ginseng ice tea, thinking "How bad could it be? It is at least wet and sweet." It was the worst thing I ever tasted. I did not even finish it. I should have poured out the tea and filled the bottle with water from the sink in the restroom to have another canteen but I didn't even think to do so.

We sat around talking and still waiting for something to do. One of the guys, who had been unusually quiet the whole afternoon, spoke up asking for an estimate on how long we would be there before going home. It was not an unreasonable request, except maybe in the context of what was going on. He was not in a position to see the questioning looks some of the other guys gave him. I tried to lighten the situation a bit by saying, "Home? We're in the army now. We may never get home!" I considered telling them that the Federal Government had nationalized the New York City Fire Department and made us part of the armed forces, but I didn't think they would buy it. The others smiled at my answer, and it relieved some of the rising tension.

INTO THE NIGHT

We stayed on the second floor for a while but then got tired of waiting around. We decided to go out and see what was going on. The boxes of food were still there and before leaving I rummaged through one and came up with a Hershey bar. It was like finding gold. I put it in my shirt pocket to save for later, and then donned my gear and joined the others who had gone downstairs already. The lobby was still crowded with firefighters. Generators and portable lights illuminated the area. I ran into firefighter Greg McEnroe of Ladder 175 while going through the doors out onto Broadway. We had been firefighters back in Engine 332 before he went "across the floor" to 175. Greg is a tall, husky guy with curly hair. Years ago he tended bar

William Groneman (under red arrow) at the command post on Broadway and Ann Street. (Photo by Steve Spak.)

Jimmy Ferretti and Al Merk of Engine 308 (lower right, "308" on helmets). WTC Building Five burns behind them. (Photo by Steve Spak)

Wreckage of Tower One from West Street. The spire of the Woolworth Building can be seen to the east at center. (Photo by Gerald Cereghino)

Fire Department and other rescue workers amid the wreckage. (Photo by Gerald Cereghino)

West Street from above, looking north. (Photo by Gerald Cereghino)

Signs of the pre- and post 9/11 worlds converge on Church Street. (Photo by Gerald Cereghino)

The famous and now controversial cross in the rubble of Building Six.
(Author's collection)

The remains of Tower One from West Street. (Author's collection)

Billy Groneman and Jimmy Esposito. (Author's collection)

Engine Company 308 and its neighbors' shrine. (Author's collection)

Engine Company 308: (L to R) Firefighters Kevin Crosby, John Ostrick, Chris Simmons (without helmet), Mark Presti (blue helmet), Randy Rodrigues, Jimmy Ferretti, Captain Bill Groneman, and Firefighter Matt Swan (Ladder Co. 117, detailed to Engine 308). West Street at World Trade Center, September 17, 2001. (Author's collection)

Captain William Groneman in front of the wreckage of the North pedestrian bridge, with the Lone Star flag which had been raised over the Alamo on September 11. (Author's collection)

FDNY patch, World Trade Center bolt, The Lone Star Flag and the photo. (Author's collection)

At Ground Zero, September 11, 2002. (Author's collection)

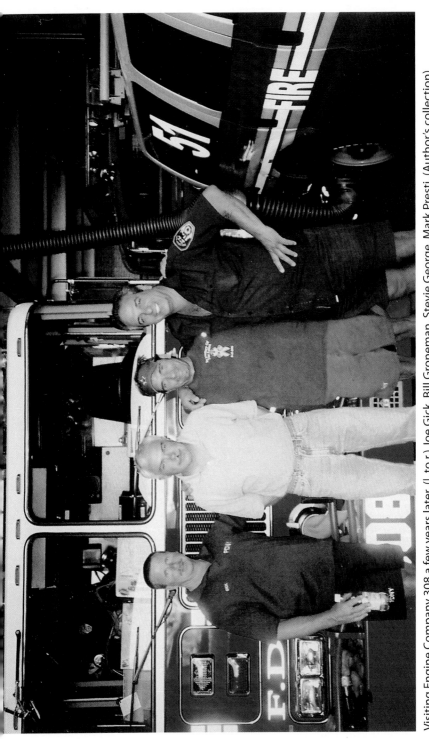

Visiting Engine Company 308 a few years later. (l. to r.) Joe Gick, Bill Groneman, Stevie George, Mark Presti. (Author's collection)

Jones Beach. (Author's collection)

in a place called MacArthur Park in Rockville Center, Long Island. I had gone there to see him a couple of times. Now, he lived further out on the Island. We talked for a few minutes. He spoke of another firefighter from 175 who had found Chief of Department Ganci's body earlier. It was a sad verification of one of the earlier rumors.

I bid Greg good luck, told my guys to wait near the front of the Woolworth Building, while I went to the command post. The post had been moved a bit north to the south corner of City Hall Park. It was just about twilight now. As I walked toward the post one of the chiefs looked at my helmet and said, "Hey Cap, do you have a company with you?" I said I did and thought, "It's about time!" He told me to round them up and relieve another engine company at their apparatus. There was an officer (I don't remember if he was a captain or lieutenant) from a Brooklyn engine company standing by. I think it may have been Engine Company 247 but I am not sure of that now either. I told him to wait there until I got my guys.

Once we were organized we followed him a few blocks south on Broadway. His company was supplying water to a tower ladder (a ladder company apparatus with a bucket equipped with a Stang nozzle at the end of a telescoping boom, instead of an aerial ladder). They had been operating there for hours and needed a well-deserved break to get some food and rest. We walked down Broadway and turned west on Cortland Street. The smoke and dust conditions became worse as we walked. In addition, darkness fell by the time we got to the apparatus. Once again it was like a descent into hell in *Dante's Inferno.*

Their apparatus was on the south side of Cortland Street about fifty feet off of Church Street. The area of the

World Trade Center was directly across Church. The smoke and dust were really bad here. It occurred to me that if I encountered smoke like this in a building I would have to put my mask (Scott Air Pack) on. We could not since we didn't have the masks anyhow. The smoke and dust also flashed crazily with the lights of the emergency vehicles. A 3 ½" (diameter) hose line was stretched into the darkness across Church Street to a tower ladder. I never did find out which tower ladder company it was, but it did not matter since the engine was not pumping water at the time.

I saw a large piece of steel of the Trade Center right across Church Street. It was a section of the outside structural steel of one of the towers sticking out of the ground. It looked like a hand reaching up out of the earth in supplication. An eighteen-wheeler had been abandoned across the street from us on the north side of Cortland. It looked dark and foreboding. There were also a couple of large pieces of steel from the Trade Center on the sidewalk across the street. The doorways and buildings on the north side of the street were all dark and dust covered. The building One Liberty Plaza loomed tall and black over us on our side of the street. It was all something out of a nightmare.

The officer gave us their handi-talkies. I don't remember if there were two or three. I would have given one to Ferretti because he was the senior man. The officer said that he and his men just wanted to take a break and get something to eat and that they would be back in about an hour. I told him not to worry about it and take all the time that they wanted. He and his guys walked away east on Cortland Street back to Broadway.

We stood around the apparatus for quite a while doing nothing. We hunched over as if we were in a storm and spoke among ourselves. Even though we were closer to the action we still were not really doing anything except manning this rig, but conditions were much more punishing.

After a while I got restless and decided to take a look around. I told the guys to stay with the rig and I would be right back. I went to the corner, turned south on Church Street, and walked one block to Liberty Street. One Liberty Plaza stood to my left and the World Trade Center block to my right. The time sequence gets a little mixed up at this point. I walked up the steps to One Liberty Plaza from the corner of Liberty and Church and then walked along a raised area outside the doors of the building back towards Cortland. It was here that I saw the only body that I was to see. It was wrapped in a white covering on a makeshift stretcher of plywood. I later heard that a bunch of young civilians were put to work hammering these stretchers together. I do not know why the body was left there. It seemed to have been forgotten. Later I saw photos in some magazines and books of a similar figure in a white shroud being carried on one of these stretchers. It may have been the same one.

The body was on my left and I stared at it for a few seconds. I was right outside a Brooks Brothers' store on the west side of One Liberty Plaza. I turned toward the store and physically jumped when I saw a number of headless mannequins standing there. I looked into the store and noticed all the expensive dress shirts stacked neatly on the shelves. The shirts were probably all nice pastel colors but now were covered with grey dust. It had the monochromatic look of a nightmare.

I went back down to the corner of Church and Liberty, and it may have been at this time that I ran into Battalion

Chief Gil Frank and Captain Hughie Mulligan. Both had their gear and dust masks on and stood on the corner talking. I recognized them by the names on the backs of their bunker coats. Gil and I had been firefighters back in East New York in the late 1970s and early '80s. He was in Engine 236 down Liberty Avenue, the same company as Jerry Migliore. He was always a decent, friendly guy. I believe Hughie Mulligan was also a firefighter in Engine 236 but I don't really remember him there. He later served as a lieutenant in Engine 332 after I had left. I think he was promoted to captain a short time after I had been. He is also a good friendly guy. I spoke to them for a few minutes and then something came up.

A fire broke out on the eight floor of One Liberty Plaza, the building outside of which we stood, and began to show through the windows. Gil Frank told me that Engine 290 was on their way up to investigate and try to extinguish the fire. Engine 290 is another company from East New York.[13]

While 290 was on its way up to investigate I returned to the apparatus and explained what was going on to the guys. I had them disconnect the 3 ½" line, which was not delivering water anyhow, and hook it up to the sprinkler connection of the building right near the rig. This would supply water to the building's automatic sprinkler system, with the hope that the fused sprinkler heads in the burning room or rooms would contain, if not completely extinguish, the fire. I also had them connect another line to the standpipe connection. This is a pipe that runs up the stairwells of high-rise buildings with hose connections on each floor or landing. Fire crews carry rolled-up lengths of hose up with them and connect off the standpipe on the landing, instead of stretching impossible lengths of hose line from the streets. We were on the opposite corner from where the fire showed, so charging the standpipe on this side may have been no help. However, we did not know where 290 would end up in the building. Whatever we and 290 did must have been the right thing because a short time after we charged the line into the sprinkler system the fire darkened down. It made us feel like we were accomplishing something.

I went back to confer with Gil Frank and Hughie Mulligan, and Gil asked me to do something for him. A civilian was with them. He had driven a truckload of diesel fuel down Church Street as far as he could go and parked a block or so north of Vesey Street, the northern border of the World Trade Center block. I do not know if the fuel had been ordered or if the driver just took it upon himself to offer it up. He was trying to find out if any of the fire apparatus needed to be refueled. Gil asked me to help the driver find out if anyone needed fuel. I walked back north with him and checked with my guys. The apparatus we were with was okay fuel wise. I do not know if the driver could have gotten further down Church Street anyhow. We continued north, passing a few other rigs, and asked the firefighters if they needed fuel, but no one did. Finally we got to the corner of Church and Vesey and I told him that I had to get back to my company. I directed the driver to the command post on Broadway and told him to take his truck over there. I walked back to my guys. The condition on Church Street, at this point, was that of a muddy, swampy mess, the result of the water mixing with the dust of the building collapses.

There was no letup from the smoke and dust. One's throat and eyes burned constantly. It did no good to sit in the rig. The air inside the cab and the riding compartment in the center was as bad as outside. At one point we gathered at the back step of the rig, broke out the engine company's medical kit, and took hits from the oxygen bottle. Other than that we just milled around and waited for something to happen.

D'Onofrio finally spoke up, saying something to the effect of, "Hey Cap., not for nothing but when I say enough is enough, it's enough." He was just verbalizing the frustration we were all feeling. I do not remember exactly what happened next but I think I suggested that he try to take a break in One Liberty Plaza. There were a set of doors on the Cortland Street side, and conditions were so bad in the street that it did not make sense for us all to be out there.

D'Onofrio drifted away into the building. In a little while he called to us, waving us into One Liberty Plaza. We found out that a triage center had been set up in the building's lobby. People were coming in for medical treatment or for a break. There was bottled water and maybe food. We all went in, but not all at once because we could not leave the rig unattended.

At some point the Brooklyn engine company's chauffeur returned. I stayed outside with him and we sat in the rig's cab. I don't think I even learned his name. We probably said no more than five words to one another. There was not much to say. The thing I remember most is the ragged burning of my throat from the toxic air.

Al Merk came out to relieve me after a while. I welcomed the break and went in and got my eyes washed out. This was done by a nurse from a hospital in New Jersey who had volunteered. We talked for a while and she told me her name. I made a point to remember her name but did not. I also got some oxygen while I was there. One thing I remember is the way she looked at me. It was the way everybody treating you looked at you. They looked deeply into your eyes as if they were trying to see inside of you.

There was a big security desk in the middle of the lobby and it almost looked like a bar. There was bottled water and soda there. I think it was at this point that I took another bottle of water and tucked it inside my shirt along with the first.

I was in the triage area at least once, maybe twice before the Brooklyn engine company came back. When they returned we gave them their radios and they took over their rig. With no other assignment we drifted back inside to the triage area. I found out the next day that this building, One Liberty Plaza, had been considered in danger of collapse. No one inside knew it at the time.

RESCUE OPERATION

I sat in a chair in the triage area. I may have gotten my eyes washed out again, or had some oxygen, or both as we considered what we should do next. We no longer had handi-talkies, having returned them to their original owners, but other firefighters around us had theirs. We heard over someone else's handi-talkie that there was a rescue operation in progress on the rubble pile. The voice on the radio requested that any available fire extinguishers (in FDNY parlance, "cans") be brought to the operation. This obviously caught our attention, especially mine when the caller on the handi-talkie identified himself as Deputy Chief Esposito.

I knew Deputy Chief James Esposito as Jimmy Esposito from Howard Beach. We had attended eight years of grammar school together. Our fathers had been best friends, and our younger brothers also went through grammar school together. Jimmy and I are graduates of Manhattan College.[14]

So, I knew that a rescue operation was in progress and that Jimmy Esposito was calling for assistance. I directed my guys to look around the lobby for any fire extinguishers, but there were none to be found. The building, or at least the lobby, had been stripped already. I took a quick look up a stairwell but did not see any. I didn't want to range any further above the first floor since I wanted us to get out to the operation. As I spoke to my guys about not being able to find any extinguishers a civilian came over. He had overheard us and he said excitedly that he knew where to get some. I asked him, "Where?" and he said there were some at a McDonald's across the street. I asked him to show me, but he volunteered to get them and raced out of the building on the Broadway (east) side. I followed him out, but lost him and had no idea of which way he went. Also, I could not spot the McDonald's. The civilian returned in a few minutes carrying two fire extinguishers. I do not know if McDonald's doors were open, if the glass was broken out, or how he got them, but he got them. He handed them over and we thanked him. I never knew his name, nor would I be able to identify him now if he was standing right in front of me.

We went out of One Liberty Plaza by the doors on the Liberty Street (south) side, turned right, and crossed Church Street to the World Trade Center block. Liberty Street, upon which the quarters of Engine 10 and Ladder 10 are located, was clogged with emergency vehicles of all kinds. To our right was the sixteen acres of the World Trade Center complex, now one giant rubble pile. Emergency workers swarmed over all. We walked about one third of the way down the block and went on the pile where there was a line of emergency workers, mostly firefighters, leading up to a crater at the upper edge of the pile. This was perhaps one hundred to one hundred fifty yards away. Jagged and twisted metal stuck out of the pile at crazy angles where ever one looked. Wire and cables were all over so one had to choose one's steps carefully. One did not so much walk as climb over everything. There were valleys and rises in the rubble. Off to the front and to the right was a giant twisted section of building lying on its side. Rescue workers climbed on this, looking into what had been windows and checking voids for possible survivors.

The area we were in, not far from Liberty Street, was brightly illuminated by portable lights powered by gasoline generators. Beyond our circle of light things were in darkness, but I could make out part of World Trade Center Building Five across the debris field to the north. Suddenly a large pink flame erupted from the building in some type of explosion and then disappeared. I had never seen a flame that color before. I and a firefighter standing next to me, looked at one another and exclaimed at exactly the same time "What the f--- was that!"

Most of the apparatus in the street were running so they poured diesel exhaust over everything. To the left, on the southwest corner of Liberty and West Streets, a high-rise building burned out of control. If this building had been burning like this under normal circumstances it would have been one of the worst disasters in New York City history. As of now, no one even attempted to fight the fire. The area in which we stood was definitely in the collapse zone of the burning building. I briefly caught the attention of Chief Esposito, who was on a rise of rubble just above me. We said hello and I pointed out the burning high-rise to him. It seemed as if the fire had just broken out in the building and I was not sure he had even noticed it. He just shook his head helplessly and said, "Yeah, Billy, I know. It's been like that all day."

Engine Company 308 stood on the rubble pile, along with many others, engulfed in the dust, acrid smoke, and combined diesel and gasoline fumes. At the time I was not even sure of the exact configuration of the World Trade Center, not having been down there in years. We were on the south side of the complex, looking north. The area to the lip of the crater was illuminated. Beyond that a portion of Building Five, still standing on the northeast corner, continued to burn, but it was not really visible through the darkness.

A rescue attempt was under way. We did not know how many victims were involved or who they were, but a rumor went around that they were Port Authority Police Officers. This proved correct. Oliver Stone later made his film, *World Trade Center*, based on this operation. We did not know how many Fire Department personnel were involved down in the crater itself. I heard someone say that it was Engine Company 290, the Prides of Sheffield Avenue, again in the action. Probably there were others too.

A line of emergency workers stretched from the street to the point where we stood, and another longer line stretched from there to the crater. Someone at the top near the crater would call for something, for example, "More Scott cylinders!... More rope!... Water!" (bottled water), and it would be relayed down the line. Then, the things requested would appear and be passed up the line hand to hand. At first a request came down and I looked down toward the street. Those further below just stared back. I found a fairly high place and yelled the request down to the street. Within seconds the requested material appeared. We had passed our McDonald's extinguishers up as soon as we had gotten there. Those at the top called for more Scott air cylinders at one point. When none appeared I climbed back down to the street to find some. Someone took me to a large rescue van from some town in New Jersey, which was sitting on Liberty Street. This person hopped into the van and handed out all the cylinders we could carry. There was no sense of accountability of private property. If it was on the scene it was going to be used if needed. I later wondered how long it took some of these other departments and companies to recover enough equipment to get back in working order.

I heard transmissions from others' handi-talkies around me. One of the most chilling I heard was somebody from the crater say, "Get a line (fire hose) down here. We've got fire all around us!" One, then another line was stretched up to the crater. FDNY fire hose are in fifty foot lengths. An incredible number were used to reach the crater. That many lengths would never be used at a conventional fire for one line, since the number of kinks, turns, and the friction loss in the line make the firefighting stream inefficient. Too much water pressure is needed, which increases the danger of a burst length. However, it was the only alternative at this operation. While we stretched one of the lines I heard someone behind me yelling, "Come on! Come on! We gotta get this line up there! Come on!" I turned around to see who was doing all this yelling. It was a young firefighter with the orange "Probationary Firefighter" front piece on his helmet. This gave me a little chuckle and I checked my collar pins to make sure I was still a captain.

At one point Jimmy Ferretti asked if we should go up to the crater. I told him no because I did not want to start free-lancing, and there were plenty of people up there already. If Chief Esposito needed us to relieve a company, he knew where to find us. I saw a few more familiar faces around this time. One of them was Firefighter Matt Swan, a proby who was detailed to Engine 308, but was originally assigned to Ladder 117, in Astoria, Queens. Swan is a swarthy little guy with a shaved head and a hyper personality, but I liked him. He is an enthusiastic and reliable firefighter. He stayed with us for a while.

I don't know how long the rescue operation went on but it seemed to take a long time. Finally word came down from the crater that the victims were on their way out. The "bucket brigade" line formed up into a double line with both lines about an arm's length apart. At least three, maybe four, orange Stokes baskets (rigid stretchers) with victims were passed from hand to hand all the long way down to the street. One victim was a heavy-set guy who had lost all of his clothing except for his underwear. He had a sort of dazed, out-of-it smile on his face as we passed him along. I vaguely remember one victim thanking people as we passed him along. One of those on the stretchers looked a bit familiar. I later realized that he was a member of Ladder 142 in my own battalion. I don't know what happened to him in the pit but the next week I saw him back working in 142, with two stress fractures of his knee supported with a brace. Normally he could have been on medical leave for weeks, if not months, with such an injury and would be fighting not to be placed on light duty. He went back to work with his injuries by his own choice. That's the way it was then.

This successful rescue took place during the late night, possibly into the early morning hours. Oliver Stone in his film took cinematic liberties and showed the victims coming down just after dawn.

Another rumor began to circulate around this time. This one involved the story of someone riding down one of the collapsing towers and surviving. First it was supposed to have been a Port Authority Police Officer and then the story changed to that it had been a civilian who had ridden down the *outside* of the building but survived with two broken legs. Over a year later I asked Matt Swan if he remembered this story and how it got started. He said it originated with the heavy-set Port Authority cop who had come out on one of the stretchers. According to Matt, someone asked the officer where he had been in the building and supposedly he answered the eighty-second floor. If he had been up that high it is unlikely that he would have survived. He had been buried for ten to twelve hours before he was rescued. Who knows if he was even rational at that point?

The idea that a civilian had ridden down the outside may have come from the fact that at least one poor soul tried to climb down the outside of one of the towers. The spaces between the exterior steel girders were only a little wider than a person's shoulders. He can be seen in some photos, wedged in a sort of fetal position between the two pieces of steel and inching his way down. Later someone said that this person was doing pretty well until the first tower collapsed and then he was gone.

As outlandish as both stories were, everyone kind of believed them at the time. You wanted to believe anything that told you someone could have cheated death amid all of the carnage.

We stayed on the rubble piles until all the victims were brought down and placed in ambulances in the street. Then we just drifted a little further up and to our left on the pile and sat down on some twisted steel beams. My "canteen" fell out of my shirt when I bent down to do something. I didn't bother to retrieve it since I could not bring myself to drink out if it anymore after it had been coated with that dust. I don't remember what happened to the other bottle. The Hershey bar had melted beyond eat-ability at that point too.

My throat and eyes continued to burn constantly. A stretched hose lines was directly to our right. One of its connections was not made up tightly and a two-foot-high geyser of water shot from between the hose butts. I took my helmet off, knelt down and washed my face in the spurting water. As soon as I did someone grabbed my shoulders and said urgently, "Brother, are you okay? Are you okay?" I got up and saw it was a firefighter whom I did not know. I said, "Yeah, I'm just washing my face off." He answered, "Oh, I thought you took a spill." I thanked him and away he went. I have no idea of who he was or what company to which he was assigned. That was the way it was. If you fell or stumbled, someone was there to pick you up immediately.

Another rumor began to circulate while we were still on the lines. This one stated that the Fire Department was going on a special schedule of twenty-four hours on duty and twenty-four hours off duty beginning the next morning.[15]

According to the rumor, half the Fire Department would be on duty starting at 9 a.m. September 12 and the other half would be off. The on-duty people would work until 9 a.m. on the thirteenth, when the off-duty people would take over. If this was the case, some of the guys with me would be on duty in the firehouse for firefighting duties at 9 a.m.

We did not know for sure so a few of the guys went off to verify this. D'Onofrio rushed back with the news. We found out that the firefighters working the following day included Al Merk, Ralph Scerbo, and Nick D'Onofrio. The rescues had been successful and everyone was just milling about at this point so I told those three to take off, make their way back to the firehouse and get some sleep. I don't know how they got back. I heard later that they took a subway to Queens and it took them a while to get back to the firehouse. I was sorry to lose Al and Ralph.

My back started to bother me while we were on the rubble pile. Every now and then I would have to lean over and rest my hands on my knees to relieve the ache. Breathing was another problem. I was having increasing episodes of shortness of breath. The smoke and dust were as heavy as ever and diesel and gasoline fumes poured over us. I was also having trouble concentrating and speaking and had difficulty formulating an answer when someone asked me a simple question.

With three guys gone, it left just me, Ferretti and, Ostrick. I was glad to have them with me. Since there was nothing going on at the moment I suggested we go back to the triage area and get another blast of oxygen. We returned to One Liberty Plaza. I sat in a chair waiting for treatment while they wandered around. I sat next to a ladder company firefighter whose name was Cleary. This caught my attention because a friend of mine, Rita Cleary, from the Western Writers of America, has a nephew on the FDNY.

For a minute I thought this might be Rita's nephew but that proved not to be the case. He had a knee injury and we talked for a while.

Eventually I was examined by a paramedic who then brought a doctor over. I filled out paperwork and they took my blood pressure, pulse, and administered oxygen. I told them what was bothering me and the doctor gave me a cursory examination. He asked me, "Is your face always this red?" I don't know how red it was but it must have been red so I told him, "No." He told me that I had carbon monoxide poisoning and not to go back to the rubble pile.

I could have easily ignored him and gone back. No one would have known. Ferretti and Ostrick returned by this point and they looked exhausted. I felt exhausted and honestly I did not know what we could have done. Things would be going on for months and we might even be back the next day. We decided to return to the command post on Broadway.

BACK TO THE FIREHOUSE

We left One Liberty Plaza and slowly walked north on Broadway back to the command post at the south end of City Hall Park. A chief was in command there but I do not know if it was Chief Haring. A handful of firefighters stood around the post. I reported in and told the chief that I had relieved three of my guys to go back to the firehouse and I only had two left. He asked me what time we had gotten there. I was still a little punchy and I hesitated in answering. Either Ferretti or Ostrick spoke up and said, "Eleven o'clock." The chief looked incredulous and asked, "Eleven o'clock?" in a way that implied "*Only* since eleven o'clock?" I guess it was about midnight or a little later by then. I still hesitated and then one of the guys added, "This morning." As soon as the chief heard that he relieved us from duty.

We found out that there were buses available to take firefighters back to Brooklyn and Queens, but no one seemed to know exactly where to find them. Someone told us to walk north to Chambers Street, where we had been dropped off that morning, and the buses either would be on the west or east end of Chambers. We walked north on Broadway again, past the Woolworth Building, and on to Chambers Street. I really did not want to walk west on Chambers. It was a long walk that would take us all the way down to the Hudson River and then the buses might not even be there. We passed a few clusters of police officers but they did not know where the buses were either.

We lucked out when we reached Chambers Street. There were a few firefighters there and I recognized one of them as Captain Jimmy Day. Jimmy and I had worked together in the old East New York days. I was in Engine 332 and he was in Ladder 175 in the same firehouse on Bradford Street. I did not know him all that well but I knew him to be a friendly guy. He has sandy-colored hair and a big round face.[16] He had one, maybe two firefighters with him. He pointed us east on Chambers toward the New York City Municipal Building on Centre Street. He said the buses were there so we walked together.

Jimmy was noticeably distraught as we walked along. He said something like, "You know, there was a time on this job when you were reasonably sure of coming home alive." His obvious implication was that this was no longer the case. He also brought up the fact that another firefighter with whom we worked on Bradford Street, Tommy Kuveikis, was one of the missing. Kuveikis or "TK" as he was known had been in Ladder 175 but recently transferred to one of the newly formed Squad companies. He was assigned to Squad 252, which had formerly been Engine 252 in the Bushwick section of Brooklyn. I had come on the job and had been in proby school with him. He was a skilled carpenter on the side and had put hardwood floors in the attic of my house in Malverne. He was an aggressive firefighter and a bit of a daredevil.[17]

There were a couple of buses waiting on Centre Street. We got on one and we were the only ones. The bus driver was black or may have been Indian. He did not say anything. An older, white-haired Irish-looking guy was also on board. He was a transit or bus company supervisor. He stood near the front and spoke with us as we left Manhattan.

I sat on the left side in the first seats that faced front. Jimmy Day sat in front of me in the seats facing the aisle. The others sat on the right-hand side. The other firefighter whose name I never learned just sat there with a barely suppressed anger. The rest of us talked quietly. There was a case of small bottles of water in the middle of the aisle. I took one.

The supervisor told us that he had been on the street near the Trade Center when the second plane hit. He said a white powdery substance started raining down almost immediately. This started a panic and stampede because people thought it might be anthrax or some other poison. He also said that at one point he looked up at one of the towers and saw three people, all on fire, hold hands and jump to their deaths together. I wish he had not told us that because that image kept creeping back, even though I had not seen it myself, and I had a tough time pushing it out of my mind, especially at night.

The ride back and the route we took were a blur. I looked out of the windows when we got back to Queens and noticed how completely empty the streets were. I never saw my city so devoid of life and movement, even during the worst blizzards of the past. It was unnerving and saddening.

Someone remarked on the significance of the date, 9/11, which they interpreted to have something to do with the emergency phone number 9-1-1. The guys kicked around the idea that the attack happened on this date for that reason. I didn't get into that conversation but while they were talking I leaned my head against the bus window and looked up at the night sky. I saw a thin crescent moon with a star very close. I recognized that to be the symbol of some Islamic nations, or a symbol of Islam itself. It occurred to me that this may have been the reason the attack happened at this time. I kept my opinion to myself.

We arrived back at Cunningham Park, loaded our stuff in Ostrick's car, and drove back to Engine 308. Once there, I took my bunker gear, helmet and hood, hosed them off, and hung them up to dry. I doubted they would be dry by later that day if I needed them. I went up to the engine office. Someone was sleeping on a cot that had been set up in there. I took a shower, changed into the clothes that I wore to the firehouse that morning, and put the uniform I had been wearing into a garbage bag to take home and wash. I probably also put on a sweatshirt from my locker because it was much cooler by then.

I went downstairs into the kitchen and heated up some leftover pizza in the micro wave. The beat-up couches in the kitchen were filled with sleeping firefighters who were due to work that morning. There was someone else awake in the kitchen but I don't remember who. The television was on and it constantly repeated the horrors of the day.

Finally I took the bag of dirty clothes, threw them in the trunk of my car, and headed home. I probably called home first to let Kelly know I was on the way. I usually did this if I got injured at a fire or came home sick from a night tour, so she would not be frightened by my entering the house in the wee morning hours.

The streets were empty. Normally if the streets were this devoid of traffic I would just drive south on Lefferts Boulevard and then go east on the Belt Parkway. However, I either heard in the firehouse or on the radio that all the roads around Kennedy Airport were closed. I took Lefferts to Rockaway Boulevard and that to the Belt, which put me east of the entrances to Kennedy. It probably took less than a half-hour to drive home.

I did not even bring my dirty uniform into the house when I got there. I set the clothes to soak in a bucket with soapy water in the driveway. Only after I rinsed them a few times the next day did I trust them to the washing machine.

I related to Kelly what went on as best I could. I had a beer and some blackberry brandy, and then went to bed. It must have been about 4:00 a.m. Very seldom had I ever dreamed about work or fires in my twenty-four years on the Fire Department, and I've never dreamed about a fire immediately after the fire. That night I had a few dreams. They were not about the terrible events of the day but every dream, no matter what it was about, was set amid the destruction of the World Trade Center.

The ocean, the sand, and the waves of Jones Beach were a million miles away and somewhere in the unfathomable past.

PART II

WHAT HAPPENED AFTER

SEPTEMBER 12, 2001

I awoke later that morning after a few hours of sleep and constant dreams set in what was already being called "Ground Zero." I drove back to Engine 308 and signed in at 12:12 p.m., fully expecting to be sent back to the site. But that was not the case. The Fire Department already had plans as to how, when, and where personnel would be deployed. There were concerns about the well-meaning but disorganized and dangerous free-lancing at the site. New York City civilian volunteers, as well as professional and volunteer firefighters from outside the city, had to be reined in. And, pre-9/11 fire protection for the city had to be ensured with less personnel and scores of fire companies out of action. Ten minutes after I arrived, Engine 308 relocated to the quarters of Engine 24, in Manhattan. A volunteer company, Engine 2-3-1 of Huntington, Long Island, replaced 308 in our quarters. The FDNY had mutual aid agreements with contiguous non-city areas, but this was the first time I had ever seen a volunteer company in a New York City firehouse.

I conferred with the battalion chief on duty and found out that members of 308 would not be going to the site as a group that day, nor would I. I stayed at the firehouse little more than an hour. At one point I stood in my office on the second floor with Battalion Chief Mike Borst. He had received a fax with a tentative list of the firefighters missing from the day before.

There is a scene in the classic John Ford film *She Wore a Yellow Ribbon*, in which Captain Nathan Brittles (John Wayne) and his commanding officer, Major Alshard (George O'Brien) sit in an office of their frontier fort and go over the names of comrades killed at the recent battle of the Little Big Horn. It is a beautifully shot scene, lighted by a deep purple sunset and scored with a soft rendition of "The Garryowen." Captain Brittles reads off some names while his eyes turn inward on a memory of each. The scene in the engine office was similar, substituting harsh reality for artistry.

Chief Borst and I stood in the middle of the sun-lighted office. He held the fax so both of us could read it. We read aloud names we recognized, mentioning our connection with the named firefighter and emphasizing our shock with some expletive. "So-and-so, I worked with him on Bradford Street!" "Oh f---! All of these guys from 105!" "I went to proby school with him!" etc. All was said in muted tones. I stood with my feet spread wide as one does when balancing oneself against weariness.

I stayed at the firehouse less than an hour, signing out at 1:03 p.m. Before I left, the officer and one of the firefighters of the volunteer company approached me seeking advice about responding to alarms in our area. It was almost funny. Huntington is on the north shore of Suffolk County, not all that far out east, but the vollies looked like big farm boys. They wore plaid shirts, blue jeans, and work boots. And they gave the impression of being coiled springs. They were not fearful in any way, but they conveyed a feeling of barely controlled excitement and responsibility.

I saw the potential of them becoming over zealous as soon as the first alarm came in, so I cautioned them to take things slowly. It was better to get to the alarm than to try to get there quickly and risk an accident. I explained the route cards kept at the housewatch desk that contained directions to every alarm box in our response district. I warned them about being alert for other units responding from different directions and finally gave a warning about drivers in our neighborhood. For some reason our area had an inordinate amount of T-bone accidents at intersections with enough force that the hit car was overturned.

I believe my friend, Gary Velilla, was around at this time. Gary and I had been firefighters together in East New York years earlier. He was now a lieutenant assigned to the 13th Division but did not have a company. During the current crisis, the Division assigned him to Battalion 51 in out quarters to help in whatever capacity he could.

There is no real way to explain Gary Velilla. Suffice it to say that he is by far the funniest individual I've ever known, in that his humor has no restraints. No matter what the situation, I would only have to see him to start laughing. But that is a different story.

It became his duty to supervise the actions of the volley company on responses. He told me later that he had to control them from taking every piece of exotic equipment off their rig and carrying with them on every run. They were certainly ready for anything.

I drove home, since I would be working the twenty-four-hour-on, twenty-four-hour-off rotation the following day. I was lost in thought about the horrible events of the previous day and probably not driving very fast in the left lane of the Laurelton Parkway, which connects New York City's Belt Parkway with Long Island's Southern State Parkway. There was a car next to me in the center lane. Suddenly, a guy driving a blue van trying to get by actually drove *between* our cars. This stupid, irresponsible act outraged me so much that I started to curse and scream at the top of my lungs. My window was open and the driver of the van must have heard me because he accelerated immediately. So did I, and the race was on. I was completely enraged and intent on catching this guy. I have no idea what I would have done, or tried to do, if I caught him. I had the car cranked up to 80 mph. He must have recognized that a maniac was chasing him because he pulled away steadily. He had to have been doing close to 100 mph around the curves of the Southern State. I gave up the chase when I reached the Malverne exit and went home. This was only the first of a number of disturbing post traumatic stress disorder incidents.

SEPTEMBER 13, 2001

I began my twenty-four hour tour at the firehouse at 9:00 a.m., Thursday, September 13. Half of the members of Engine 308 reported for duty in the firehouse.

There were about twenty-nine people assigned to 308—I, as captain, three lieutenants, and approximately twenty-five firefighters. Of the firefighters, some of our probationary men were detailed out to other companies on the proby rotation, and we had four from other companies detailed in. Everyone had been accounted for except Terry McShane, detailed to Ladder 101 in the Red Hook section of Brooklyn and now missing at the World Trade Center. A former member, Ronnie Gies, was also missing, as was Battalion Chief Dennis Cross of Battalion 57, father of Brian Cross, one of the probies detailed into Engine 308.

The normal manning of Engine 308 for fire duty is an officer and five firefighters. The rest, under the new twenty-four hour system, would be assigned to other duties. Everyone hoped it would be at Ground Zero. Things were pretty chaotic at the firehouse, and it was difficult to determine who would be assigned fire fighting duty since everyone wanted to be downtown. The firehouse was filled with those working and those going off duty. One of the first things we did was relieve Brian Cross from active duty and assign him to go home and remain with his mother.

More problems arose over who was going to work at the firehouse. One probationary firefighter, John Barone, detailed in from a Manhattan company, had a minor emotional episode in the kitchen. He believed the whole on-duty assignment of his original company had gone missing. He began to weep when I assigned him to fire duty because he wanted to be down at the Trade Center searching for them. I told him, in not so gentle terms, to get a grip on himself, and that everyone in the firehouse with more time on the job than he knew people who were missing. He finally pulled himself together. As it turned out his company was not missing.

It was a complicated day. I, like everyone else, was determined to be one of those assigned to work downtown, but I was not sure that would be the case. Our on-duty (firefighting) crew from the night before and the apparatus were still at the quarters of Engine 24 and Ladder 5 in Manhattan, covering the response area of that engine company. Engine 24 and Ladder 5 had been caught in the collapse of the towers. Many of their men were missing and their rigs were either destroyed or still downtown somewhere.

Meanwhile, my son, Billy, twenty-four years old at the time, told me the night before that he intended to go down to Ground Zero to volunteer. He worked for Costco while waiting to be appointed to the New York City Police Academy. I told him to contact me after 9:00 a.m. If I was going downtown he could come with me and work with the 308 group.

A minor mutiny arose as I gave out the assignments for that tour. Everyone on duty wanted to be assigned to the group going down to the Trade Center site, and no one wanted to work regular firefighting duties in the firehouse. I certainly planned on going. The on-duty guys of Engine 308 assembled at the front of the apparatus floor. I assigned Lt. Bob Urso to be the officer on duty in the firehouse, Jimmy Ferretti to be his ECC, and four other firefighters to man the rig. Urso and Ferretti immediately and adamantly refused, saying that they were going downtown.

I don't know how long we debated the issue, but I was learning that what I wanted as company commander did not really impress anyone that much. Finally I relented and said that I would stay in the firehouse, and that Bob Urso would be the officer going to the site. I told the rest of the guys to work it out as to who would go and who would stay. Seniority counts a great deal in the FDNY. If no one stepped up and volunteered to work in the firehouse, I planned on ordering the junior ECC and the four junior firefighters to stay, and that would be it.

I went back up to the office for a few minutes and Bob Urso followed me. He felt bad about how things had gone on the apparatus floor and now he volunteered to stay back, allowing me to go. I declined. I told him to go, and I would go the next time. I was not angry at all, and I wanted him to know that. There would be plenty of chances for all.

Things worked out by the time we came down. Mark Presti, a senior man and ECC but not a regularly assigned chauffeur, volunteered to stay. He would drive. Probationary firefighter Matt Swan, detailed from Ladder 117, and John Barone, both on Proby rotation, stayed, not that they had the slightest say in the matter. I got John Ostrick and Kevin Crosby to stay by telling them I could use them and putting them on a guilt trip.

So, we finally had the crews figured out. The slightly larger crew would be available for duty at Ground Zero, and six of us would work fire duty in the firehouse. It was not as simple as that. The crew available for World Trade Center duty could not go directly to the site. Instead they had to go to our Division 13's quarters, which were a mile or so to our northeast, to await assignment and transportation.

The crew on fire duty had nothing with which to perform fire duty. Our rig and last night's crew, Lieutenant Cliff Payan and five firefighters from yesterday, were still on duty at Engine 24 and Ladder 5's quarters in Manhattan.

We had expected that after the change of tours some other unit would be sent to replace 308 in Manhattan and then 308 would return to Queens. That did not happen, however, since the department was spread too thinly. We found out that those of us on fire duty had to go into

Manhattan, relieve our guys on duty, and remain on duty there until further orders. It was up to us to figure out how to get there. Luckily, Mark Presti drove a large van. Better still, it was red and it could accommodate the whole crew and our gear. Mark offered it for our use. We would drive it into Manhattan and the off-going crew would take it back to our quarters. We finally got rolling in Presti's van at 11:30 a.m.

Many of the major highways in the city and all accesses to Manhattan were still closed to non-emergency vehicles. I can't remember the exact route we followed, but I remember flying along on some highway in Brooklyn, probably the Brooklyn/Queens Expressway, or maybe the East River Drive in Manhattan, and holding my fire helmet out the window to identify us to the police along the way.

Engine 24 and Ladder 5 are located at Houston (pronounced "House-ton") Street on the southern edge of Greenwich Village and about a mile north of the World Trade Center. These companies took a bad hit in 1994 when they lost three members at a fire. Captain John J. Drennan, (L 5) and Firefighters James F. Young (E 24), and Christopher J. Siedenburg (E 24) died from injuries sustained at a fire caused by a plastic trash bag left on a kitchen counter near a stove top. Their deaths began a string of tragic fires throughout the city in which twenty-two firefighters and fire officers died in the line of duty over the next seven years. Now Engine 24 and Ladder 5 were dealing with a greater tragedy.[18]

We heard a strange news report on the radio during the drive in. A woman claimed that she had received a cell phone call from a group of six firefighters trapped inside the wreckage of the World Trade Center. They survived the collapse, according to the story, by climbing into an SUV in one of the parking garages. This set into motion a great deal of effort in trying to verify her story and locating the trapped firefighters.

We arrived at 24 and 5 and relieved 308's crew from the day before. They turned over their handi-talkies and Presti handed them the keys to his van. I and the guys with me were now on duty as Engine 308, acting Engine 24.

An air of subdued confusion reigned at 24 and 5. The firehouse had men missing at the World Trade Center and both companies were out of service. I believe the engine company's apparatus had survived the collapses but it was not in condition to be put back into service yet. A very sad and stressed lieutenant of Engine 24 labored to restore some order to the chaos. Other members of both companies must have been there too, but I was barely aware of them. We replaced Engine 24, and Ladder 52 from way north in the Riverdale section of The Bronx acted as Ladder 5.

Some family members of the missing had gathered at the firehouse waiting for word of their loved ones. They remained out of sight in either a room or a courtyard behind the firehouse. A couple of chefs from one of the local Greenwich Village restaurants volunteered their services to keep an excellent buffet going in the kitchen for the comfort of all.

The atmosphere of the firehouse was that of a church. I explained the situation to my guys and suggested that we stay out of the kitchen unless we wanted to grab a bite to eat or a cup of coffee. Everyone readily agreed. We generally stayed at the open apparatus door or at the house watch area. I was in and out of the engine office a few times.

My main contact in quarters was the lieutenant from Engine 24. He was the first one I saw when we had arrived.

I told him the story we had just heard on the radio of the firefighters surviving in the SUV. His face broke into a disbelieving smile. The survivors could be the guys from his house. The news later turned to be a bitter disappointment, however. The story was a hoax. I felt sorry I relayed the tale, giving the lieutenant some false hope. The woman who made the call was later found and prosecuted. I believe she was sentenced to a year in jail. I don't know how much of that she served, but whatever it was, it was not enough.

We from 308 leaned against the front bumper of our rig, speaking softly among ourselves. The apparatus door stood open and we walked out occasionally and looked up and down the block. The corner of Houston St. was to our left. A crowd of people stood behind police barriers there. In front, a deserted Sixth Avenue led directly south to the smoking ruins of the Trade Center.

I paced around restlessly from the apparatus floor to the engine office, to the house watch, and to the front of the firehouse. It was on one of these walks outside that something truly amazing happened.

I walked out front and glanced around when I heard, "Dad! Hey Dad!" I recognized the voice before the words even registered. It was my son, Billy, calling from the crowd on Houston St.! He had seen me and tried to get through, but a conscientious police officer wouldn't let him. I went over, dumbfounded that he would be there. He and his friend Andre, a co-worker from Costco, had taken the subway into Manhattan with the intent of volunteering at the Trade Center. Many subway stops had been closed under and around the Trade Center, so Houston St. was the closest they could have exited the system. Of the hundreds of stops in New York City, he ended up getting off the subway right where I had been sent!

After I got over the shock, I brought Billy and Andre through the police barricade and into the firehouse. I explained the situation to them and told them that they weren't allowing any more civilian volunteers down to the site. They were disappointed but agreed to stay with us at the firehouse. I felt proud that they wanted to volunteer and felt a little bad that they weren't going to be able to. I walked with them a block or so south of the firehouse to let them get a little closer look toward the Trade Center, but all we could really see was the still seething cloud of smoke. In a way, I was also relieved that they would not be going down there. It was a dangerous and toxic place and they had no training or protective gear.

Another civilian showed up when we got back to the firehouse. He claimed he had escaped from a building across the street and just south of the World Trade Center. He insisted that there were people trapped in an elevator of that building and that he knew where to find them. I don't know how he got through the police lines. The police may have brought him to the firehouse themselves. I took his information, tried to piece his story together, and had him point out on a map where his building was located.

In the middle of this we had our first and only run while acting Engine 24. I told Billy and Andre to stay put and we responded. The run was for a gas leak in the street at Lispenard and Church Streets. This was the same gas leak to which Engine 7, Ladder 1, and Battalion 1 responded on the morning of September 11. These units had two documentary filmmakers, Jules and Gedeon Naudet, riding with them at the time. The Naudet brothers captured on film the first plane plowing into Tower One.[19]

We arrived at the location, noted the odor of natural gas, and informed the dispatcher. The dispatcher was already aware of the leak and it seemed as if there was some type of street excavation nearby which may have been in response to, or may have caused the leak. We did all we could. There was no danger and the small leak would have to continue until the utility company, Con Ed, could spare a crew to mitigate it.

I asked Mark Presti to drive by my brother's building, 346 Broadway, so I could see if he was around. It only occurred to me when we got there that everything in Lower Manhattan was shut down and Michael wouldn't be there anyway. Broadway was closed to non-emergency traffic and for a while we actually drove north on southbound Broadway, one of the most famous streets in the world.

We returned to Engine 24 and Ladder 5. The civilian was still there and I had another session with him trying to piece his story together. I also contacted the dispatcher trying to find some way of getting him down to the scene. Finally, either the police or a Fire Department messenger took him in a department Suburban. I know I tried both. In retrospect I do not know if the guy was on the level, was nuts, or was working some kind of angle to get down to the site for reasons of his own. I know that I could not take the chance of his story being untrue against the possibility of people trapped in an elevator for the past two days. I never heard anything after that about people being found in an elevator.

Engine 24's apparatus eventually returned to the firehouse, covered with grey dust and missing some tools, but relatively undamaged. Some members of Engine 24 worked on it to restore it to firefighting readiness.

I conferred with the on-duty lieutenant several times. His brother, who was a correction officer somewhere, showed up and I spoke to him outside the firehouse. He told me that the lieutenant had been in one of the towers before the collapse and that he and a few guys went one way to get out and the others went another. The guys who did not go with him did not make it out.

By late afternoon, the lieutenant told me his apparatus was ready, and he had enough men to go into service for fire duty. The only hitch was that he had only one handi-talkie and a minimum of two was needed for fire duty. An officer and his engine company chauffeur each needed one to coordinate water delivery at a fire. He tried to get another handi-talkie but his efforts were in vain. The solution was simple. I gave him one of our three handi-talkies. These radios are tightly controlled on a division level. Normally, loaning one to another company in another division, no less, would cause a bureaucratic headache of tracking and accountability. However, things were different now and we had greater nightmares with which to deal. I and the lieutenant took marks in the office record journal and the house watch journal and that was it. He notified the Manhattan dispatcher and Engine 24 went back into service as a firefighting unit. The dispatcher notified Engine 308 to return to our own quarters a few minutes later.

I told Billy and Andre that we would take them back to Queens. The only problem was that now there were eight of us, but only six riding positions on the rig. Billy said that they would take the subway back. I didn't want them to go all the way back on the train and it was still too close to the event to completely feel comfortable with the subway system—another prime target for terrorism.

FDNY engine apparatus have six riding positions—two in the cab for the chauffeur and officer and four in the riding compartment in the middle of the rig. These are positioned two facing forward and two backward on each side of the engine. It is cramped quarters. We all tried to figure out how to squeeze one more person on each side.

Someone suggested that a couple of the guys could ride the back step. I quickly dismissed that idea. The back step is a small platform on the rear of the apparatus. Firefighters step up on this when removing hose from the higher hose bed. Years ago it served as a riding position. As many as four firefighters bounced along on the back step responding to alarms and in an immediate position to stretch a hose line. Safety considerations during the department's "War Years" of the mid 1960s to the late '70s called for this position to be eliminated. Firemen on the back step were too easy targets for projectiles and even gunfire. However, tradition dies hard on the FDNY. "The back step" is still used to refer to a firefighter who does his job honorably throughout his career without aspiring to promotion or any assignment other than firefighting, i.e., "He was on the back step at engine so-and-so for twenty years."

Tradition notwithstanding, I was not going to let two guys ride the back step over highways all the way back to Queens. Finally, John Ostrick and Matt Swan volunteered to ride up on the hose bed. This also was unheard of, not to mention unprofessional. However, in light of the things that had happened in the past week, existing rules had to bend a bit. So, they climbed up on top. We put Billy and Andre on the backward-facing seats on either side of the engine. Crosby and Barone took the jump seats at the doors and off we went.

Presti eased the rig out of quarters and turned left. We had to go through the barricade and crowd on Houston Street. We were not prepared for the emotional reaction of the people. They went crazy. They cheered, yelled encouragement and thanks, and waved signs and flags. Engine 24 and Ladder 5 are located on the southern fringe of Greenwich Village. The traditional, and perhaps stereotypical, view of the people there is that of avant-garde bohemians, culturally aloof from the rest of New York. The display of emotion belied all the stereotypes. Almost everyone in the city or the whole country wanted to do something to help at this point, but were limited in what they were able or allowed to do. For the citizens of this part of Manhattan their role was to stand on Houston St. and throw everything into an emotional outpouring for our benefit.

It was difficult not to get caught up in the whole thing. The guys, including Billy and Andre, waved back and thanked them. I took a small paper American flag that someone had placed on the dashboard and waved it out the window. The crowd cheered and we moved east on traffic-crowded Houston St.

I asked Presti to make a right on the Bowery and then left on Delancy Street. I wanted to show Billy the Lower East Side, the area in which my father had been a fireman. It is an area bordered by Chinatown and Little Italy, and where many languages, including Yiddish, can be heard on the streets. We turned left on Delancy, passed Allen Street and gave a symbolic acknowledgement down toward Canal Street, where the quarters of Engine 9 and Ladder 6 are located. My father was a fireman in Ladder 6 until the late 1970s, when cancer forced him onto light duty. He lost the final battle in August, 1980.

The lads from 9 and 6 had plenty to think about and be thankful for at that point. Four days earlier the crew from Ladder 6, under the command of Captain Jay Jonas, had been in a stairwell of Tower One when the building fell. They had halted their evacuation to help a civilian, Josephine Harris. All were in the vicinity of the fourth floor when Tower One let go. Miraculously, they, Ms. Harris, and a handful of other firefighters all survived the collapse. They managed to get out hours later, only after discovering that they were not sealed in and that there was open sky above them rather than one hundred stories of office building. Had they not stopped to help Ms. Harris they would have been further down in the stairwell or perhaps outside, where certainly all would have died.[20]

We continued east on Delancy St., over the Williamsburg Bridge into Brooklyn and on to Queens. We brought Billy and Andre to Howard Beach, the neighborhood where I had grown up, and where he then lived in an apartment with his mother.

My mother lives in this same neighborhood in the same house she has lived in since 1932. She grew up there, and my brother and I grew up there, as well. We passed her house, continued a few blocks down 99th Street, and dropped off Billy and Andre. My mother's husband, Mikey Novak, ever vigilant at the front porch window, spotted Engine 308 as we went by the house. He and my mother immediately "turned out" and overtook us before we left Howard Beach. We had a short meeting on 100th Street in sight of my alma mater, Our Lady of Grace Grammar School, where I gave them a rundown on everything that was going on. Following this debriefing we returned to the quarters of Engine 308.

We found out later that the crew from 308 who had gone to the division never did get sent down to the Trade Center site that day.

SEPTEMBER 15, 2001

Thirteen of us again reported for duty at Engine 308 on Saturday morning. Bob Urso was to be the officer on duty in the company, with five firefighters. The rest of us were held in reserve. Lieutenant Cliff Payan and a group working the night before at the Trade Center returned to quarters at 12:00 p.m. What happened next is not clear but at 12:45 Bob Urso and a group of firefighters left to go to Division 13 for duty at the Trade Center. I assumed firefighting duties at the firehouse along with Ferretti, Ostrick, Swan, Rodrigues, and one other. Mark Presti was assigned to the battalion as the chief's aide. Kevin Crosby was an extra man and assigned to office duties.[21]

A few conversations and incidents come to mind at about this time, but I cannot be sure that they happened exactly on this date. They did happen during tours I worked at the firehouse right after September 11.

One was a conversation around the kitchen table at 308. One group of firefighters had been back to the site already. Wayne Slater was one of those who returned to quarters with Cliff Payan on the fifteenth. I asked Wayne, a senior man, how bad the conditions were. He spoke of the conditions and of finding a firefighter's boot which was filled with water and seemed to have some gelatinous mass in it. I didn't feel the need to pursue that any further. In the course of his descriptions he concluded, "And Cap, the stench of death is everywhere."

Battalion Chief Kenneth Grabowski of Battalion 51 sat at the table at this or maybe some other gathering. He also described his impressions and some things he witnessed. He said, "They caught some guy taking watches and jewelry from the corpses in the morgue." Everyone stopped and listened. Chief Grabowski added, "The cops beat the piss out of him." Everyone nodded in silent approval as if to say, "Of course, what else could they do?"

Another incident stays in my mind involving an alarm to which we responded, possibly on the night of the thirteenth. We responded north on Lefferts Boulevard but the alarm turned out to be nothing. It was after dark, but the intersection of Lefferts and Liberty Avenue, a terminus of the A-Train subway line, was teaming with traffic and people. I noticed a car in front of us as we approached this intersection on our return. The car was filled with young guys and it was moving very slowly. The young guys held a large flag out of the window. I did not recognize the flag but it certainly was not American. I think it may have been an Afghani flag, but I am not sure. With the lights of Engine 308 directly behind them, the occupants of the car looked around apprehensively. I noticed people on the street looking at them and then at us, as if wondering what would happen next. The car cruised slowly. I do not know if they were trying to goad us, or if they were just afraid of making a wrong move. Finally they went on their way without incident and we returned to the firehouse.

Engine 308 is quartered at 107-12 Lefferts Blvd., in the borough of Queens. It is an area where three New York City neighborhoods, Richmond Hill, Ozone Park, and South Ozone Park come together. Traditionally these neighborhoods were ethnically German, Italian, and Irish. The demographic had changed by the dawn of the twenty-first century. The area around the firehouse was now populated predominantly by Indians and Guyanese. Some, but not many of the Indian population, wore traditional turbans. Needless to say, the customs and ethnic practices of the local population were a bit different than those of the members of 308, which reflected the earlier demographic. This had never been a problem before, but in the wake of September 11 there was potential.

Another earlier session around the kitchen table brought the matter to the surface. One firefighter stated something to the effect that, "I don't know if I'm going to be able to do things for the people around here anymore." I explained that the locals were predominantly Indians and Hindus, not Middle-Easterners and Moslems. But, I went on, that was not our call to make and we would continue to do our jobs serving the citizens of New York City regardless. It became a non-issue, though. We continued to do our job and the local population proved very supportive.

There was a small mosque on a side street just off Liberty Ave., not far from the firehouse. I was not sure if there was going to be any trouble there. We drove by and I saw an American flag prominently displayed. I never noticed one there before. There may have been one. I just don't remember seeing one.

SEPTEMBER 17, 2001

The department organized itself into a routine based on the newly established twenty-four hour on-and-off schedule. The normal amount of personnel (one officer and either four or five firefighters) still worked in existing companies in fire duty capacity while the rest were available for assignment at Ground Zero.

My first opportunity since September 11 came on the seventeenth. A group of us from Engine 308 were to go by bus with a few other companies from our battalion to the Trade Center and put in a ten-hour day.

The plan was this: we, the members of Engine 308, were to provide our own transportation to the quarters of Engine 285 and Ladder 142, and from there a bus would take us to downtown Manhattan. Engine 285 and Ladder 142 are two other companies in our division, sharing a firehouse less than a mile and a half west of 308. Their south Queens neighborhood, like ours, is a cramped mix of private homes, small apartment buildings, and a variety of businesses. Parking is at a premium under the best of circumstances.

With that in mind I asked the battalion if it would not be better for the bus to come to our quarters first, pick us up, proceed to 285 and 142, pick them up, and then continue west to Manhattan, thus eliminating the added concerns about parking. I was told that this was no good. The instructions came from the division and the division wanted it done according to the original plan. So, I suggested an alternative where the bus picked up the guys from 285 and 142 then swung east to 308 and then downtown. This idea also did not fly. I had forgotten I was dealing with a system I sometimes referred to as "the bureau of bureaucracy."

It was no big deal. We squeezed into a couple of cars and/or vans and went to 285 and 142's quarters. There were eight of us. I had Mark Presti, Jimmy Ferretti, Randy Rodrigues, Mark Simmons, Kevin Crosby, John Ostrick, and Matt Swan, all good men, with me.

We boarded the bus, mingled with the teams from 285 and 142, and waited impatiently to leave. Finally, we were on our way, or I should say the *driver's* way. Instead of pointing the bus west toward Manhattan, the driver immediately headed east. No one questioned him since we all assumed there was some purpose to the route he chose. We assumed incorrectly. I and everyone else were delighted to see that in less than five minutes we passed directly in front of Engine 308's quarters—the place at which we could not be picked up. The "bureau of bureaucracy"—you know!

The driver was not a member of the Fire Department. He seemed to be of a recent third-world vintage. I assume that he was a New York City bus driver and that we were on a city bus. I could be wrong. Maybe the city chartered busses and drivers. Either way I soon became amazed that the driver was permitted behind the wheel of a bus or any other vehicle.

Tensions were understandably high among the firefighters. It did not help matters when the driver proceeded south on Lefferts Blvd., bypassed the westbound lanes of North Conduit Boulevard and the Belt Parkway, which would have taken us toward Ground Zero, and turned east on South Conduit. Firefighters know what they are doing in their profession and they generally extend that assumption of knowledge to others in theirs. However, when the bus turned south on the Van Wyke Expressway and into Kennedy Airport, some gentle consternation arose from the passenger section. "Where the f--- is he going?" "Does this guy have any idea of what he's doing?" "Hey driver, where are you going?" etc. The driver remained oblivious and drove us deeper into the maze of airport roadways. Either he was a total incompetent or else he did not want us to get to Ground Zero.

I may have been the only captain on board and as such, the highest ranking firefighter. I felt it incumbent to express our collective dissatisfaction to the driver and perhaps nudge him toward a more westerly route. I said something to the effect of, "Take the next exit and turn this f---ing bus around and do it now!" I also managed a tone conveying that it would be in the driver's best physical interest if he changed course immediately.

While I was voicing my route suggestions, one of the funnier guys from Engine 285 tramped to the front of the bus in his bunker pants and had a private conversation with the driver. I had to laugh as the firefighter turned in the aisle, paused dramatically before returning to his seat, and rolled his eyes upward in a manner that said, "We are dealing with a moron here!"

Despite the driver's best efforts, we were soon on the Belt Parkway westbound to Manhattan. Trucks and buses are not permitted on New York City's parkways, but we took it anyway. Maybe the driver finally sensed our urgency to get to the scene, or maybe he knew no better anyhow.

We traveled from Queens into Brooklyn along the Belt, with Jamaica Bay on our left. Everyone spoke quietly during the ride except for one firefighter from either 285 or 142 who sat directly behind me. He kept up a sort of nasal, nonstop chatter most of the ride. He owned some type of construction company and pointed out some marine cranes in the distance that he owned. He then touched on the subject of whether or not the World Trade Center wreckage was contaminated with asbestos. The official word was that it was not. He announced, "They say it's not an asbestos site? Let me tell you something, guys—it's an asbestos site!"

Finally, he turned to the subject of how the whole operation was being run by the higher-ups. His take was that they were going about it all wrong and, apparently, he was the only one who knew how it should be done.

It was typical firefighter griping, and maybe I should have ignored him and let him go on. However, it was impossible in the close quarters of the bus, and tension levels were rising. I turned to him and said, "You should tell them that. When we get down there you should go right to the command post and explain to them how they are doing it all wrong." That brought him up a bit short. He had some kind of answer, but his nervous chatter slackened off after that. I took no satisfaction out of this brief exchange, and I wasn't trying to throw my somewhat limited weight around, which wouldn't have gone too far anyway. This story and the previous one regarding the inept bus driver have little to do with the big picture other than illustrate that nerves were wearing thin.

We continued on past Sheepshead Bay, Coney Island, Bay Ridge, and under the massive Verrazano-Narrows Bridge, which connects Brooklyn with Staten Island. Here the Belt becomes the Shore Parkway and the Leif Ericson Drive. We followed the roadway around the southwest edge of Brooklyn, where it connects with the Gowanus Expressway, then on through Red Hook, and the Brooklyn-Battery Tunnel into Lower Manhattan.

We exited the bus on West Street south of the World Trade Center wreckage. My memory gets a bit blurry at this point. I have no idea of what became of the guys from 285 and 142. I and the crew from 308 made our way to the north entrance of the World Financial Center on Vesey Street, but I am completely blank on how we got there.

Vesey Street was the northern border of most of the World Trade Center complex. Only Building Seven formerly stood on the north side of Vesey. The World Financial Center stands just west of the World Trade Center complex across West Street. A pedestrian foot bridge above West St. had connected the two centers, but it had been destroyed in the collapses.

We arrived at the entrance of the Financial Center on Vesey, just off West, and saw a small cluster of firefighters and officers around a deputy chief who was issuing orders. I reported in seeking an assignment but was told to "stand fast." It would become a familiar scenario. From our position on West Street most of the view of the Trade Center was blocked by the Financial Center building. The buildings comprising the Financial Center suffered damage, but it was amazing that they were still standing in light of what happened just across West Street.

A rough plywood structure stood just west of us on the sidewalk and into Vesey St. I saw it but didn't take much notice of it. I assumed it housed some type of street excavation. I did not inspect it closely and never questioned whether or not it was there before the attack. While outside on Vesey, I also became aware of a foul odor which permeated the air.

Since we were not assigned right away, nor did it seem we would be anytime soon, we sought a place to sit down for a while. I and the boys from 308 entered the World Financial Center into a mall lined with restaurants and a bar, all of which opened directly into the mall. They appeared to be a little more upscale than your average lunch places. Of course they were all closed. Hastily abandoned might be a better description. Vertical trays of dough stood in a fancy pizza place, with the white dough dripping and hanging over the sides of the trays. I then thought I had figured out what the foul odor was. All the food in those eateries had been spoiling for the past week, and no garbage had been removed.

We passed a bar on the right, with all its bottles lined up and inviting on open shelves. We nodded hello to the police officer who stood at the entrance guarding the trove. We exited another set of doors at the south side of the mall into an open area which looked out onto the Hudson River. The guys settled at a table in this pleasant area. It was difficult to imagine the great destruction just on the other side of this building. I told them to stay together and remain there while I went back out to the street.

Too much time has passed to put everything down as it happened. I believe it was around this time that I saw a bit of commotion toward West Street. I looked over and saw a group of big firefighters carrying a Stokes basket. Besides using it to transport victims, the FDNY often uses these stretchers to carry equipment. As I watched them approach I wondered what they were carrying, and why all of them were crying.

This involves a couple of generalities I came to believe during those days. One, like seeing the smoke around the top of the Trade Center on September 11, is that one has difficulty recognizing things out of context. The other, as I was experiencing now, is that one sometimes refuses to recognize things that one does not want to.

Had I seen a photograph of this I would have recognized it immediately as firefighters carrying a body, wrapped in a black body bag, on the Stokes. They were the men of Rescue 1, one of the elite Rescue companies, and they were carrying one of their own. They were led by Battalion Chief John Norman, who was also noticeably distraught and crying. I knew John from the old East New York days, when he had been one of the Sheffield Avenue crew. He was now a battalion chief assigned to the Special Operations Command. I avoided making eye contact with him at this time.

I found out a short time later that they carried the body of Joseph Angelini, Sr., of Rescue 1, which they had just removed from the rubble. Angelini was one of, if not the oldest, active firefighters on the FDNY. He had forty years on the job and was still on hard active duty in Rescue 1. He had been off duty on September 11 but like everyone else had rushed to the scene. Besides his devotion to duty and obligation to the people of New York City he had another concern that morning. His son, Joe Jr., was on duty with Ladder 4. The sad truth is that both father and son perished in the collapses.

I looked away from the approaching members of Rescue 1 and finally came to recognition of other things. Three chaplains stood outside the plywood structure, and I realized that it was actually a makeshift, temporary morgue. Then, Wayne Slater's words about the "stench of death" came back to me, clearing up the mystery of the foul odor permeating the air.

Rescue 1 brought Joe Angelini's remains into the morgue and I hung around the deputy chief waiting for an assignment. After a while the chief told me to get my company because he wanted us to bring out a firefighter. I rushed back through the mall and found the guys where I had left them. I told them to get their gear on, that we had assignment, and "…a grim duty it is, too." I fully expected to be sent up on the rubble pile to remove the body of a firefighter, but I was wrong. The chief hadn't made himself clear or else I misunderstood. He wanted us to form an escort to remove Joe Angelini's body from the morgue to an ambulance, through a street side opening on the opposite side.

We entered the morgue, and if I had been unconsciously not recognizing things, now I was consciously trying not to recognize. I remember six or so tables or stretchers to the right, arraigned in a semi-circular fashion. There was a dark mass on each, maybe a black body bag, maybe not. I caught this in my peripheral vision and purposely did not look any more directly or closely than that initial glance.

An EMS team had Angelini on the ambulance's rolling stretcher. There was no formal protocol for what we were doing, so I led the way, with the others from 308 either behind me or following the stretcher. It was a short walk out the street side to the ambulance. We may have helped load the stretcher and/or we may have done a hand salute. I do not remember now.

The rest of the day became a blur. We worked on several "bucket brigades" on the West Street side, passing five-gallon plastic buckets of debris from various parts of the site to a location where it could be inspected, then removed. Just to take stock—the World Trade Center complex consisted of seven buildings covering sixteen acres in Lower Manhattan. Two of the buildings were the towers, one hundred ten stories in height, and each floor an acre of office space. I have referred to the "rubble pile." It is important to remember that this pile covered the sixteen acres. In some parts it reached to a height of seven to ten stories, maybe more. This is not to mention the seven basements or sub-basements below the Trade Center and the buildings on all sides of the complex that suffered damage. And we were removing debris with five-gallon plastic buckets.

The lines of bucket brigades moved and shifted, as was the case near the FDNY's West Street command post of September 11, near a loading dock of the World Financial Center. One minute it was going strong, then a few guys drifted away, and then a few more, and the line either petered out or shifted its focus a few yards away.

Originally, the filling of buckets was color coordinated. Grey buckets were for debris and orange ones were dedicated for body parts. The line shifted from the loading dock to the right near the wreckage of the pedestrian bridge to the Financial Center. This bucket brigade went up a high mound of debris. Empty buckets went up and full ones came down. Someone at the top of the line announced "body part," and after a while an orange bucket went up.

As the bucket came down the line I felt compelled to look into it. I felt I had to in order to condition myself to things that surely were to come. On the other hand, it seemed like a voyeuristic invasion of someone's private dignity. The bucket reached me and I reluctantly glanced inside. There was something in the bucket about the size of a hand. However, it was wrapped in what looked like a plastic bag and impossible to identify. I passed the bucket on without looking any closer.

We probably stopped to get something to eat during the day. Some type of small cruise ship had been docked at the marina on the Hudson River. It was set up as a rest station for rescue workers, with food, medical, counseling, and even massage services. We may have gone there for something to eat.

Later, after dark, we worked on the debris pile on the Trade Center side of West Street. Engine 308, and guys from other companies concentrated on an area where a big section of the exterior structural steel had fallen. Guys dug in the grey-yellowish dust between the steel members of the grid-like wreckage.

After a while someone again announced "body part." I looked over and only saw a small, maybe inch-square, piece of jellied matter in the dust. At this point I don't know if it was due to the darkness, the fact that I wasn't wearing glasses, or because I was psychologically blanking out things that I didn't want to see clearly.

The space between the formerly vertical steel members was a little more than shoulders' width. Randy Rodrigues of 308 crawled into one of these spaces and dug into the dust below. I noticed him brushing the dust with the flat of his hand rather than digging. He stopped suddenly and looked up with a perplexed, shocked expression on his face. I looked over and saw that he had uncovered the smooth, bright red surface of a fire apparatus. Others digging below the steel reached windows of the rig and were able to see that they had reached the riding compartment. At first it seemed the rig had turned over on its side. Later we determined that it was still upright on its wheels, but the body above the chassis had collapsed sideways. Someone reached into one of the windows and brought out one or two Scott face-pieces, from which we were able to identify the apparatus as that of Engine 10.

The word was that once anything Fire Department related was found, a command post had to be notified. The command post would send a chief over to supervise. It may have been intended for the finding of remains of firefighters; however, I thought this was important enough.

Also, I did not know how many guys may have been missing from 10 and if any may have been with their rig.

I asked a firefighter, not of Engine 308 but one who was working in the same area, to go to the command post and let them know what we had found. He was standing closer to the street and not actually doing anything at the time. He looked back at me with a blank stare. I asked him again—still nothing. Finally I took the face pieces, climbed from the pile, passed the firefighter with the blank stare, and went to the command post about fifty yards away on West Street. I believe a battalion chief came back to the area with me. Engine 10 did lose three men, but none were found in the area of their apparatus.[22]

Sometime during the late afternoon or early evening, I walked back through the restaurant mall in the World Financial Center. There I ran into Billy Esposito. Billy is the younger brother of Deputy Chief Jimmy Esposito and a firefighter in Rescue 4 in Queens. Billy grew up with and went to grammar school with my brother Michael. Billy was always one of the toughest and strongest kids when we were growing up and into adulthood. Among the many stories associated with him in the old days was his ability to open a beer can by squeezing it and to be able to eat a whole pizza by himself. I never saw him on or off the job when he didn't have a big smile on his face, especially when potential danger was looming. As I saw him now he looked sad and lost. I spoke to him for a while and invited him to join my group if he wanted. I asked him if he was okay and he answered, "You don't understand, Billy, these were my best friends." He was referring to the members of his company and the others of the elite rescue community lost. There was nothing I could do for him or say to him. I left him standing in the mall. I don't think I ever saw him since. It was a bad way to leave an old friend.

We stayed downtown about ten hours that day. Before we left, the members of 308 assembled at a point on West Street. We sat on pieces of Trade Center steel, waiting for some direction as to where we would catch buses back to Queens. A female police photographer walked by us and stopped to take our picture. We also asked her to take a picture using one of our cameras.

Later we caught a bus a couple of blocks north on West Street. Luckily it was not the same driver as that morning.

THE FIREHOUSE

Engine 308, like all the other firehouses in the city, reeled in the aftermath of September 11. The company had a missing member, Terry McShane, as well as a recent member, Ronnie Gies, and the father of detailed member Brian Cross. Some companies, such as Manhattan's Rescue 1, had lost as many as eleven. Other firehouses, which housed two companies, lost more between them. However, there was not a company in the city not affected. Almost everyone in every company either worked with or had known someone who was gone.

An impromptu shrine soon appeared outside 308's quarters. A sign asking others to "Remember our missing brothers" was constantly supplemented by offerings from the neighborhood in the way of candles, flowers, and cards.

September 19 saw another change in the Fire Department's work schedule as the chart changed from twenty-four-hours-on—twenty-four-hours-off to twenty-four-on—forty-eight-off. The Department also initiated a "task force" system to rotate firefighters to the scene. As usual the guys adjusted accordingly. They fought fires and responded to other emergencies; attended funerals; fulfilled their responsibilities as spouses and parents; dealt with the attention focused on them; mourned the loss of co-workers; friends, brothers, and sometimes fathers or sons; and returned to dig in the rubble of Ground Zero.

PTSD

This narrative follows no precise chronological order from this point on due to the passage of time, the erosion of memory, and the need to make some observations on certain subjects. One of these is post traumatic stress disorder, or PTSD.

This term is used most frequently in regard to combat veterans returning from overseas. At the time it was not applied so readily to emergency service workers. I saw it manifested in me the morning of September 12 in the incident where I chased the van on the Southern State Parkway, but I did not yet recognize it for what it was. I saw it among the normally affable guys of 308, where tempers suddenly were on the point of eruption. One incident which seems trivial now comes to mind.

One of the guys took great pride in the job and Engine 308. He always put together multi-photo picture frames of fires and other emergencies to which 308 had responded and hung them in the firehouse. Of course, if someone in a firehouse shows interest in something it almost becomes incumbent upon some others to mess with it.

Somebody took the frames and rearranged them, or moved them around the firehouse. It was just a bit of firehouse nonsense, with no damage to the frames or photos. I sat in the kitchen while the firefighter became uncharacteristically angry and confrontational with others over the prank. The other firefighter involved seemed to take undue satisfaction in his reaction. The whole exchange became very annoying to me. Finally, the victim of the prank turned to me and said, "What about this, Cap?"

The argument was totally trivial and unusual. More unusual was that the firefighter appealed to me or any officer to try to solve it. I felt myself losing my temper— also unusual. I explained in a low, modulated voice that I thought the whole thing was nonsense and that we had bigger fish to fry, and I left the kitchen. My remarks were not directed at any individual, but everyone. They are all great firefighters and great guys. We were all a little nutty at the time.

The FDNY's Counseling Unit had their hands full along with everyone else. They quickly put together and sent a training video on PTSD, to all firehouses to be viewed during the twice-daily drill time. The video listed all the signs of PTSD with a brief explanation of each and how and where to seek help. As the film ticked off the different symptoms—inability to sleep, nightmares, drinking, loss of appetite, disinterest or inability in sex, loss of temper, etc., some of the guys responded in typical firefighter fashion by saying, "Yes… yes… yes..." as each symptom appeared on the screen. Some of the more imaginative fell back on an old mantra from childhood when trading baseball cards, "Got it… got it… need it." We were joking, but we knew the problem was real and it was there.

One very ugly scene played out some time later and I was at the center of it. We received an alarm for a building in Kennedy Airport. Of course, in the wake of September 11 everyone's adrenaline began pumping as soon as the airport was mentioned. We responded with lights and sirens by our usual route, south on Lefferts Blvd. Cars were parked on both sides of the street, there was traffic on the opposite side, and a double-parked milk truck blocked our way. The driver of the truck was making a delivery at one of the local stores. I blew the air horn and waved at him to move the truck. He responded by stepping into the oncoming lane and waving us around his truck. Even without traffic in the other direction it would have been a tight squeeze.

We were losing response time now. I continued to blow the horn and began yelling to him to move the truck. He ignored me and continued to wave us around. I lost it. I struggled to extricate myself from the seatbelt, jumped out of the rig, and ran to the driver. I got right in his face and screamed at him as loud as I possibly could, using every foul word I could think of. I don't know what I said. I may have threatened to have him arrested. I may have threatened to kill him. Luckily for me he did not respond in any way or I probably would have attacked him. The guys on the rig were so stunned that no one moved. After a few seconds of insanity I climbed back in the apparatus. The driver moved his truck and we squeezed by. I was still so crazed that I hurled an obscenity at him again as we passed.

We never did get to the airport. The alarm turned out to be nothing and we were turned back. I think we may have gotten as far as the Belt Parkway, which is the northern border of JFK. I rode back to the firehouse slumped over in my seat. I was in the lethargic shock that follows rage. We returned via Lefferts Blvd. I looked for the milk truck, fully intending to apologize to the driver but he was gone already.

The guys were all quiet when we returned to quarters. No one said anything to me or each other. They were like children who have just watched one of their parents go berserk. I think I managed an apology to them when we got back.

My actions were a disgrace to me, Engine 308, and the FDNY, and it was totally my fault. That's the only time something like that ever happened to me while working and I'm glad it never happened again.

DREAMS

One of the sidebars to PTSD is dreams. I was not troubled by constant bad dreams immediately after the attack. I did have trouble falling asleep. Every time I lay down at night, images of the events of September 11 played out in my mind. I had particular trouble imagining the absolute torture the people trapped on the four jets went through. Thoughts of the planes streaking toward the towers from the perspective of people in the towers, and the thoughts of people jumping or falling to their deaths from a quarter mile high also haunted me. I tried to think of other things while going to sleep, but these thoughts always crept back. The only way I managed to cope was by imagining that I was physically pushing these thoughts behind a door, forcing the door closed.

I could not control the dreams that came a bit later. There were only a couple but they were enough. In one I walked down a foreboding New York City street at night. I looked to my right at a dark recessed doorway and saw Terry Hatton step out in full firefighting gear. Stunned by his sudden appearance I said, "Terry, you're alive?" He looked at me with a sad, sympathetic smile and said, "Billy, you know I'm not alive." At that another firefighter in gear walked up from the left and spoke quietly to Terry. Their conversation excluded me. They were obviously in a place or a state that I was not. I woke up from the dream at that point, shaken.

Two nights later I dreamed that I was sitting with friend Gary Velilla, normally a situation that would set the stage for some of his crazy antics. We were in a high, cavernous building. The interior was all green wood and there was some type of fire department drill going on involving apparatus operating inside the building. Gary and I sat in chairs talking while a young firefighter walked by. Gary gestured at him with his head as if he was going to make one of his jokes. Then I saw another person walking from right to left along the wall behind us. He was turned halfway toward the wall as if he did not want to be recognized. I saw that it was Vernon Cherry, a firefighter I did not know but knew of, who was missing at the Trade Center. Gary and I stood up and I said, "Vernon, is that you?" He stopped walking and turned slowly toward us smiling enigmatically. As he faced us his head remained smiling at us but his clothes and lower body faded into tattered black rags that blew in the wind.

I woke up with a sustained scream that had to have lasted a good twenty seconds. The following morning I made an appointment to speak to someone in the Fire Department's Counseling Unit.

I visited the unit and spoke to one of the counselors there. He assured me that the dreams I had were typical of persons who have lost someone. Just speaking about this to someone helped because the dreams stopped as suddenly as they began.

Another benefit from visiting the counseling unit was that I came face-to-face with Firefighter Kevin Flaherty of Engine 238. The last time I had seen his name was on the list of the dead and missing that Battalion Chief Borst shared with me in my office on September 12. Kevin had been thrown over some turnstiles in the lobby of Tower One when Tower Two collapsed. He had gotten out and been in the street when Tower One came down. He tried to run, but his back had been injured and he stood almost paralyzed in the street as he was enveloped by the dust and debris. Luckily he made it. This was another case when I actually told someone that I was glad to see that he was alive.

FOUR FIVES, AND FUNERALS

The FDNY announces the line-of-duty death of a member by transmitting signal 5-5-5-5. A tone comes over the voice alarm followed by the dispatcher announcing, "It is with regret the Department announces the death of firefighter …." The four 5s come from the days when telegraph keys were used. The dispatcher would tap out a series of fives, four times. Maybe we would receive this sad announcement twice a year. In bad years it has been as many as six or more. In 2001 we had already heard it six times prior to September 11. The Department suffered a terrible loss just three months before on Father's Day when firefighters Harry S. Ford (Rescue 4), Brian D. Fahey (Rescue 4), and John J. Downing (Ladder 163) were killed at an explosion and collapse at an intentionally set fire in a commercial building. Eight children became fatherless on Father's Day. At the time it seemed nothing could get worse but it did.

Funerals have a long tradition in the FDNY, a job that requires them in sometimes alarming frequency. Approximately fifty firefighters had died in the line of duty since I had come on the job in 1977. The FDNY is the only department in the country that has one engine apparatus specifically dedicated to service as a funeral caisson. It is not unusual to see firefighters from as far away as Los Angeles or Dublin in attendance. Volunteer fire departments on Long Island are especially helpful when FDNY funerals are held in their towns, providing manpower, the use of their rigs, meeting halls, and facilities. Firefighter deaths are a tragic and traumatic occurrence touching everyone on the job. The closer one is to the epicenter of the tragedy, the more severely one is affected.

The Department's Emerald Society Pipes and Drums Band always plays at funerals, regardless of the ethnicity of the deceased. The size of this world-renowned band ranges anywhere from fifty to seventy-five members. Following the church service, they escort the casket on the Fire Department caisson down the block to a point where it is transferred to a funeral hearse for its trip to the cemetery. The band solemnly plays the dirge, "Going Home." Once the transfer is complete, the band triumphantly and powerfully marches back to the church playing a rousing tune like "Garryowen", imbuing the rest of us with the strength to go on.

A collation usually follows the solemn duties of the funeral. These gatherings of firefighters with food and drink can only be described as an Irish wake on steroids.

Fire Department funerals are emotionally, physically, and psychologically draining. The Department, besides the responsibilities of normal fire protection and intensive search efforts at Ground Zero, was now faced with the potential for three hundred and forty-three funerals.

In the beginning I told myself that it was important to attend every funeral. Of course that became impossible both physically and mentally. Then, I thought I would attend as many as I could. In the end my participation in wakes and funerals became hit and miss. If one pushed oneself to be at every funeral, the affect on mind and spirit probably would have been permanent.

One of the first wakes was that of Firefighter Ray York. I attended on duty with Engine 308 since Ray's wake was held right in our area of Ozone Park. Ray was from Howard Beach, the neighborhood in which I grew up, but I never knew him. He was assigned to Engine 285 in our battalion but was working light duty at the Fire Zone, a fire safety educational facility in Rockefeller Center, on September 11. He had injured his shoulder months before, and was a few weeks away from retirement. He got to the Trade Center that morning by hitching a ride on a passing ambulance.

I ran into an old friend, Paddy Connolly, also of Howard Beach, there. Paddy is a few years older than I, and from one of the great old Irish families of the neighborhood. I started hanging around with him in the early 1970s, when a group of locals would gather on cold winter Saturday mornings to play touch football in the Our Lady of Grace schoolyard. We played softball on the

Malone's Bar and Grill team during the summer. Paddy is a third generation New York City firefighter. Since then his oldest son followed in his footsteps. Paddy went on the job in the class before me, in 1977. I've always looked up to him as an older brother.

Another early wake was that of Battalion Chief Cross. A group of us from 308 met at the funeral home and stood in a long reception line to pay our respects. While waiting in line I noticed Jerry Tracy, also a captain and with whom I had attended Proby school. I didn't speak to him as he was sobbing in tears as he walked by.

Mrs. Cross greeted each of us and exchanged a few words as we came up to express our condolences. Brian was by her side. She was very strong, and that is the way it was. The families, those most affected by the tragedies, bolstered the rest of us by their pure courage and strength.

Another wake was that of Joe Vigiano of the NYPD. Joe was a son of Captain John Vigiano (retired), one of the most renowned fire officers of the FDNY. The Vigianos suffered the terrible blow of losing both of their sons on September 11. John Vigiano II was a member of Ladder 132. Once again, the Vigianos' quiet strength when greeting people was a thing to behold.[23]

After the wakes came the funerals, and sometimes memorial services. I attended that of Battalion Chief Ray Downey (also known as "God"), on December 15, on Long Island.

All FDNY line-of-duty funerals and memorial services always have more uniformed attendees than can be accommodated in the church. The common practice now is to have a loudspeaker system for those outside to follow the service. I remained outside at Ray Downey's service along with many others. One person who was not in the church was Chief Downey himself. He had not been found.

Following the service I was briefly interviewed by Steve Dunleavy, a writer for the *New York Post*. I happened to be standing there and he saw me and came over, asking for some memories of Ray Downey. I related my story of him as an instructor in Proby school. I don't know if my comments ever made it into print.

It may have been before this service that I walked through the church parking lot and ran into Deputy Chief Phil Burns.[24] I had the privilege of working with him when he was the captain of Engine 332 for a time in the early 1980s. When I met him in the parking lot, he was changing into his uniform of an Emerald Society drummer to play at the service. As we were talking, Battalion Chief Jim McKenna (retired) walked over. He had followed Phil Burns as captain of 332, and I also worked with him there. He is definitely one of the toughest guys I've ever known. It occurred to me that I was talking to two of the best firefighters and fire officers on the job, and I had been lucky enough to serve with both of them. This happened at one of the funerals or memorials services, but as usual, I am at a loss to remember which one.

TASK FORCE

As stated earlier, the Department again changed its work duty chart on September 19, adjusting it to twenty-four-hours-on—forty-eight-hours-off. I worked twenty-four hours at 308, from 9 a.m. Wednesday, the nineteenth until 9 a.m., Thursday, and then the same thing beginning at 9 a.m., Saturday, the twenty-second. The Department also set up a task force system for assigning personnel to the Trade Center site. Our turn came during the week of September 24.

I and a team from 308 were assigned four ten-hour shifts that week. Our first assignment began at 1:30 p.m. and ended at 11:30 p.m., Monday, September 24. This day was significant to me since it was the twenty-fourth anniversary of my entry into the Fire Department.

Members from companies in the borough of Queens drove to a marina on Flushing Bay, right across from Shea Stadium, at that time the home of the New York Mets. Tents had been set up at the marina where everyone could get something to eat before leaving by bus for downtown. There was also a large tent set up on a pier where firefighters could pick up any basic equipment or clothing they needed. I took a few items I thought I could use—plastic goggles, kneepads, a small flash light, extra gloves, a tee shirt, etc.

I had found a small athletic bag belonging to Kelly in my garage at home. I took this and fashioned a shoulder strap out of a piece of clothesline and carried it with me. It came in handy since I was able to put the small items from the supply depot in it.

The department also issued brown overalls to be worn in lieu of the heavy bunker pants. Firefighters would still wear their helmets (or construction helmets), bunker coats, and boots at the site. The overalls were supposed to be turned in upon returning to the marina and clean ones issued each time.

The mood at the staging area was fairly tense and somber. Many members were strung-out and tired, but everyone was anxious to get down there and work. The women and men who served the food buffet-style were very friendly and upbeat. I was fortunate that Gary Velilla was there with me. We sat together and had something to eat. He provided some subdued, but much needed, laughter with his usual crazy banter.

Once the department accounted for everyone assigned according to company, we boarded buses and headed downtown. This time the ride was much more organized and direct.

We arrived on West Street a few blocks north of the Trade Center. As we exited the buses we were quickly organized into a formation by Fire Department officers already on the scene. An ambulance drove north from the site as we were called to attention and ordered to "Hand salute!" It carried the remains of one of three hundred forty-three firefighters. The formation broke up and everyone turned south, walking quietly toward "Ground Zero."

Engine 308 fell in with two other companies from our bus as we walked down West Street. I fell behind, lost in thought about the ambulance and the formation in which we had just taken part. I thought *Is this the way it is going to be?* We had not been there a minute and had stood in an honor formation for a firefighter of whose name we were not even aware.

As a result of my musings I reached the command post at West and Vesey Streets slightly behind the other two officers. We lined up in front of the deputy chief in charge of the post. He looked at the first officer and assigned him and his company to report to a certain sector and go to work. He looked at the second officer and did the same. He looked at me and said, "And Cap, you keep your men here in reserve."

"What?"

I was not happy and neither were the guys from 308. I let the chief know that we were not too thrilled with our assignment. He assured me that we would be given something to do.

A large white tent had been set up on West and Vesey to serve as the command post. It had phones, radios, maps, equipment, water, some food, and a large box of assorted candy and energy bars.

I and the guys stood or sat around outside the post looking toward the site, which was across Vesey and to the left of West Street. Most of the debris had been removed from West St. between the World Financial Center and the wreckage of the World Trade Center by then. However, the street was filled with equipment, such as cranes, trucks, generators, piles of heavy timbers, etc.

Rescue workers from a variety of services—firefighters, police officers, state troopers, FBI, construction workers, military, and many others swarmed over the sixteen acres of wreckage searching for signs of life but mostly, at this point, bodies. The burned out remains of World Trade Center Building Six stood darkly and ominously on the northwest corner of the site, blocking most of our view. One large mountain of wreckage was visible from our position, and more as we moved around a bit.

Engine 308 did receive a few assignments, but only in support of things actually going on in the wreckage, and all of it after dark. We carried a generator and some lights around and later stretched a 3 ½" diameter hose line to Engine 24, which was back in operation. Engine 24 supplied water to Tower Ladder 35, operating on West St. Mostly we waited around.

At one point the chief had me answering phones and radios in the command post tent. I let the guys drift over to the wreckage to see what they could do, with the understanding that they keep in some kind of contact with me in case we were assigned something as a unit.

Deputy Chief Jimmy Esposito walked up to the command post sometime during the night and conferred with the chief in charge of the post. I had the opportunity to speak to him briefly while standing on the traffic island just outside the tent entrance. It was the first time I had seen him since the night of the eleventh. Almost everyone was carrying a camera of some type by this time. I had a disposable one with me so I asked one of the guys from 308 to take a picture of Jimmy and me. We stood with our arms over one another's shoulders as we may have done thirty-five years earlier in the Our Lady of Grace schoolyard. It was the first photo we had taken together since we received our Confirmation into the Catholic Church in the spring of 1964.

Units drifted to the command post as our ten-hour tour wound down. We walked north and boarded buses on West St. for the ride back to Flushing Marina. The bodies of at least three firefighters had been removed from the rubble that night.

Our assignments for the rest of the week worked out as follows: we were assigned from 9:30 p.m., Tuesday, to 7:30 a.m., Wednesday; we returned on Thursday, from 5:30 a.m., to 3:30 p.m., and finally from 1:30 p.m. to 11:30 p.m. on Friday, September 28.

At this point it is impossible to remember everything that happened during the rest of the week. Notes I had taken at the time are woefully inadequate. The same pattern of assembly and transportation from and to the marina was followed. The staggering of hours added to the whole surreal atmosphere and to the present confusion about times and events.

Frustrated by our lack of assignment on Monday afternoon, I was determined to do something about it. I felt the fault was mine after slowly strolling down West St. and arriving third at the command post. I stepped up the pace on Tuesday night, striding purposefully toward the post. The officers lined up again with me in the center position.

The chief looked to my right at the first officer and assigned him and his company. He looked to my left and assigned the third officer and company. He then looked at me and assigned Engine 308 to reserve. Once again we were not too happy.

We did receive a few assignments. For a time we monitored debris removal by crane at the intersection of Greenwich and Barclay Streets. This involved visually inspecting the removed debris for human remains. We did not find any.

Later, the chief had us act as a FAST unit. FAST stands for Firefighter Assist Team. This unit, usually a ladder company, is designated by a chief at a fire to stand fast in a position to immediately assist any firefighter injured or trapped. The unit is kept out of the actual firefighting and stands near the command post with a Stokes basket filled with tools, rope, etc., that would assist them in their rescue.

We set up on West St., looking out over sixteen acres of skyscraper wreckage. I'm sure there were other units around the other three sides of the site with the same assignment. Luckily, no searcher on the debris got into any trouble which required a rescue. The tour ended without much happening and we were back at the marina by 7:30, Wednesday morning.

We returned at 5:30 a.m. on Thursday. This time I raced down West St. once our buses arrived. I reached the command post first, with the other two officers coming up behind me. The chief looked at the second officer and assigned him. He looked at the third officer and assigned him. He looked at me and told me to hold my guys in reserve.

My thoughts strayed toward assault and battery at this point, but instead I followed the chief around, remonstrating about the situation and his lack of awareness that my guys had to do something for the total effort and for their own sense of contributing. He responded with more bland assurances that we would be given something to do.

I think I gave it up psychologically at that point. I don't remember what the next day's assignments were like. Sometime during Thursday or Friday we were given the exciting job of helping to move a supply depot of equipment that had been set up on the second floor of the World Financial Center. We hauled the stuff down to trucks. Where it went or why it had to be moved I have no idea. It was not exactly the kind of work for which we had hoped.

RANDOM EXPERIENCES AND OBSERVATIONS

The intervening ten years have blurred much of what happened during the last week of September, 2001. Certain memories of people, places, and events stand out, but even these may be uncertain as to time. For instance, I remember standing at the command post when a flash of color on a passing rescue worker's shoulder caught my eye. It was a Lone Star flag of Texas. Its wearer was a captain of the Houston Fire Department, leading a FEMA team from Texas. I followed him over to the north side of Building Six where his exhausted team rested. Some of them actually slept on the sidewalk right alongside the burned-out building. I spoke to the captain and a few of his people about my impending move to Texas within the next year. We visited for a while and I had one of his men snap a photo of us, along with a female firefighter of his team. In my memory this clearly happened in the dark of night. However, in looking at the picture recently I saw that it had been taken in what appears to be a feeble daylight. It had to have been taken just after dawn on either the morning of Tuesday, the twenty-fifth, or Thursday, the twenty-seventh. In light of the "faulty warpy reservoir" of memory as described by Steinbeck, I will recount a few observations, in no particular chronological order.

FOOD

There was no shortage of food for rescue workers at the site and elsewhere. I recall sitting with the members of Engine 308 against a concrete traffic divider on West St., fairly early on our first day there during the task force phase. A couple of young people came up with a box of wrapped hamburgers, or chicken sandwiches, from a local restaurant and handed them out to each of us. They were very good, not just as food but due to the "we're all in this together" thought behind the gesture.

Food was available on board the ship docked in the marina on the Hudson River. A steady stream of rescue personnel entered and exited this vessel. Stations with running water had been set up on the dock so workers could rinse off the Trade Center dust from their boots before boarding.

Manhattan Community College campus, a few blocks north at Murray and West Streets, also provided food. We availed ourselves of that site at least once.

My thanks go out to all the institutions, restaurants, and volunteers who kept us well fed during our time there and at the staging areas such as the one at the Flushing marina.

WRECKAGE AND DEBRIS

As stated a number of times, the World Trade Center wreckage field covered sixteen acres plus of Lower Manhattan. The debris consisted of the wreckage of the two one hundred-ten-story towers, the twenty-two story Marriot Hotel (Building Three), nine-story South Plaza Building (Building Four), the burned out and partially collapsed nine-story North Plaza Building (Building Five), the eight-story U.S. Customs House (Building Six), and the forty-seven story Building Seven. In addition to these there was the partial wreckage of buildings on all four sides of the site and hundreds of vehicles.

The pile rose as high as ten stories in some places, maybe higher. It went down seven stories *below* street level into the sub-basements of the complex. A wall of the exterior structural steel stood on the north side of what had been Tower One. Three large sections, probably from

Tower Two, stood where they had speared into West St. toward the south. Rain had fallen a couple of times since the eleventh, mixing with the all pervading dust to form an almost muddy soil.

Heavy equipment had replaced our original five-gallon plastic buckets for debris removal. Cranes, powered shovels, and dump trucks were everywhere. I looked on with awe as parts of a giant crane stood on eleven flatbed trucks to be assembled on site. I was told that the tool at the end of the crane alone cost three-quarters of a million dollars.

The wreckage still steamed and smoked. Irritating fumes of burning metal poured from many places in the pile. Pieces of steel, still cherry red from heat were pulled from the wreckage for weeks after.

As I looked upon the mountains of wreckage and the debris itself, I saw no clear signs that what I was seeing had been office buildings. Both towers had 110 floors, each with an acre of occupied office space. Yet nothing in the debris was readily recognizable as office equipment or furniture. I have heard other firefighters say the same thing. A number of firefighters also observed that you did not see a piece of concrete bigger than a football.

I only recall seeing two pieces of office material in the wreckage and that was during my last day or two there. I looked down at one point and recognized the swivel wheel of an office chair. Later, I looked up at a broken street-sign post. The steel post had been broken off and an office chair seat was impaled on it. I tried to imagine the force which caused this without causing the light seat to simply bounce off the jagged post.

A couple of other pieces of debris or articles stay in my mind. Somebody brought a license-plate-sized piece of aluminum to me while I was at the command post. It had a row of rivets on it which identified it as a piece of the fuselage of one of the jets. I brought it to the attention of the chief at the post and asked him what we should do with it. He answered, "Throw it in the dumpster." I asked him if it wasn't needed as evidence. He replied, "We know what happened to the planes." Good point. We got rid of it. We should have kept it.

Another artifact was on a more human level. We had received some duty on Friday night, our last night there. We operated on the edge of the debris field on West St. I looked down and noticed a woman's shoe in the dust. It was black with a kind of chunky heel, and it was lying on its side. I thought about the care its owner probably had taken on the morning of the eleventh to coordinate a pair of shoes with whatever outfit she would be wearing that day. I tried not to think of where she may have been at that moment. I hoped that the loss of a shoe was the only thing its owner suffered.

A couple of chiefs stood nearby. I pointed out the shoe to them and asked if we were recovering things like that. I thought that perhaps DNA could be taken from it. One of the chiefs answered, "Is there a foot in it?" When I replied in the negative, he said, "Then forget it."

The last artifact was a piece of one of the buildings. A steel bolt caught my attention while I crossed West St. on one of my last two days there. I picked it up and put it in my bunker coat pocket. It probably came from the exterior steel grid on one of the towers. It is approximately 5 ¼" inches long, 1" in diameter, and its hexagonal head is 1¾" wide. It had been cleanly sheared off at its threads. I walked a couple of steps and saw another slightly longer bolt of the same kind. I thought briefly of how the two bolts standing on end side-by-side would resemble the two towers in miniature and might make a fitting memorial display. Maybe that image kept me from picking up the second. Maybe I just didn't want to carry the added weight. Either way, I didn't pick up the second one.

One symbolic article that I brought *with* me to the site was a Lone Star flag of Texas. It had been sent to me by my friend Dorothy Black of Texas. Dorothy is a member of the Daughters of the Republic of Texas, the organization entrusted with the care of the Alamo.

The Alamo's gift shop offers for sale Lone Star flags which have been run up the flag pole at the Alamo. On the morning of September 11, Dorothy and other members of the DRT had a number of flags raised briefly over the Shrine of Texas Liberty. They sent one to me because of my long time involvement with the history of the Alamo. I was told later that the others were sent to President George W. Bush, New York Governor George Pataki, New York City Mayor Rudolph Giuliani, Fire Commissioner Thomas Von Essen, and Police Commissioner Bernard Kerick.

I received it by mail earlier in the week, wrapped the folded flag in plastic, and carried it in the makeshift athletic bag at least two days at Ground Zero. I wanted to record its presence there, so I had one of 308's guys, I believe it was Tom Lynch, take my picture holding the flag.

It was in the early morning after sunrise, probably on the twenty-seventh. I stood on the south side of the wreckage of the north pedestrian bridge. I removed the flag and held it, folded, as Lynch snapped the picture. A number of rescuers carried personal flags and banners to the site. The word was that those in charge did not want everyone unfurling and flying flags there.

Most people there probably did something like this to record or commemorate the momentous event in which we were involved. However, everyone remained cognizant of the horrendous human loss and was respectful to the site and the collection of human remains.

The "stench of death," as described by Wayne Slater, permeated the air and got worse. At one point, and I can't remember when this was, I stood on West Street when a group of firefighters, carrying a Stokes basket containing a body bag, approached from the south. They were still a good thirty feet away when the odor hit me. I recoiled as if I had been struck in the face.[25]

Later, I stood by the wreckage of the pedestrian bridge with a battalion chief. He was an older Italian guy who smoked a small cigar. I did not know him personally. We searched around the area and he mused, "What are they going to do with all this steel?" I answered, "Make bombs out of it." He laughed a bit at that. Then, he turned to the subject of the bodies. "We know they're here," he said, "You can smell them." He was right. A short time later, searchers found a body, or parts of a body, on top of the pedestrian bridge near where we stood.

CELEBRITIES

Everyone wanted to help. Many people, regardless of whether or not they were rescue workers, rushed to help when the attacks occurred on September 11. Many office workers in Lower Manhattan refused to leave and pitched in to the early rescue work. Emergency service people from outside the city and outside New York State rushed to the scene. Civilians served food, collected and distributed necessary material, and donated blood. Consistent across American culture was the desire to do something to help.

Many notables also answered the call in any way they could. In some cases they served food at certain staging areas. Others came to the scene as morale boosters and mingled with rescue workers. Their visits were appreciated. Celebrities needed to know that they also were doing something to contribute.

I heard that actress Susan Sarandon served hamburgers at the staging area in the Jacob Javits Center to the north. I saw actor and comedian Nathan Lane on board the ship at the Hudson Marina. He worked the crowd and kept spirits up. I did not get the opportunity to speak to him there. I think I saw actor Kevin Bacon there, too.

Famous folks also braved the dust and foul conditions to show up at the West St. command post and other places around the site. One was Ronan Tynan, the famous Irish tenor. He approached the command post one night with some official. Being an Irish music fan, I recognized him immediately. He walked up and shook hands with me. It was like shaking hands with a cinder block.

The chief came out and the official introduced Mr. Tynan. The chief, apparently not an Irish music fan, mistook him for someone in officialdom whom he had been expecting. Once the confusion cleared up they entered the tent to talk.[26]

Ronan Tynan is a great friend of the FDNY and it was a pleasure to have met him there. A few years later he became an American citizen. He also sang at the funeral of President Ronald Reagan.

Another night, or maybe later that same night, the New York Yankees arrived. Derek Jeter, Tino Martinez, and others suddenly appeared and mingled with firefighters at the command post. Manager Joe Torre probably was not far away. I would have liked to see him since he is my mother's younger cousin and I had not seen him in about thirty years.

My mother is a great fan of then Yankee Tino Martinez. I spoke to him for a few minutes and had firefighter Joe Gick of 308 take a picture of us. A framed copy of the photo now sits on the radiator cover in the front porch of my mother's house in Howard Beach. I, in turn, took a photo of Joe with Derek Jeter

Word spread fast about the Yankees, and a group of EMS workers surged up. One was a young, attractive female EMT or paramedic. I recognized her as an instructor for the firefighters' Certified First Responder program, which she taught in a bored, lackadaisical manner. Later she worked in headquarters and I would see her sitting in her cubicle there. I never remember seeing her actually working in the field. I never knew her name. She always had a sort of aloof surliness when it came to firefighters. It was interesting to see her appear then, almost at a run, and all bubbly and girlish because Derek Jeter was on the scene.

A home-grown celebrity made an appearance, also at night. I stood outside the command post, looked to my right and realized former fireman Dennis Smith was standing next to me. Dennis became famous in 1972 when his novel *Report From Engine Co. 82* propelled him from the firefighting to the publishing world. He has since gone on to write and publish a number of books, both fiction and non-fiction, and found *Firehouse Magazine.*

I spoke to him there for a while, mostly about our common interest in the printed word. His book *Report From Ground Zero* appeared in 2002. It is very good despite containing what I considered to be at least one factual error, which will be explained later.[27]

I'm sure there were other notables on all sides of the World Trade Center site—entertainment, sports, and political figures alike. They all brought moral support to the effort and all should be commended. The music and entertainment communities would demonstrate this in a more spectacular way a few weeks later.

RELIGION

Religious imagery and references were very present in the aftermath of September 11. Impromptu shrines developed outside of most firehouses, especially those housing companies that had lost members. These shrines usually were a combination of religious and secular items.

Religion was also present at Ground Zero, sometimes overt, and sometimes below the surface. Whenever human remains were uncovered a priest, minister, or rabbi said a blessing over them if possible. In the democracy of this New York City melting-pot battlefield it did not matter who was blessing whom.

Sometimes religion presented itself in strange ways. A group of us were gathered at the West St. command post one day when a young, slim Catholic priest walked up. I believe he was from the church right outside of New York City Police Headquarters at 1 Police Plaza. He approached us and asked in a calm voice if we were all right. We responded that we were. With that his face grew red and he screamed, "Well I'm not! I'm as mad as hell and I want to f---ing kill someone!" We all turned to him, shocked, and said things like, "Whoa, Father, take it easy!" He calmed down and stood with us for a few minutes. He then moved off and did the same routine for another group of firefighters walking away from the site. I understood what he was doing. He was helping us by making it necessary for us to calm him. He was also telling us that we were not alone in anything we may be feeling. He was good. I wish I would have spoken to him more. I saw a documentary on 9/11 a few years later in which a young slim priest is shown walking purposefully toward the World Trade Center during the attack. I believe it is the same priest.

Another priestly encounter occurred one morning on the west side of the debris pile. I noticed a tall, older gentleman to my left. He stood staring out over the mountains of wreckage. I struck up a conversation and he identified himself as a police chaplain. I assumed he meant an NYPD chaplain.

We spoke for a while when Lieutenant Ritchie Smioskus walked up rapidly. Ritchie was the FDNY's official photographer and ran the department's photo unit. I knew him from working in headquarters and often went to him for photographs during the time I worked as technical editor for the department's magazine, *WNYF (With New York's Firefighters)*.

Ritchie was always under a good deal of pressure. He constantly handled the photography of major fires and emergencies, department events and ceremonies, forensic evidence at fire scenes, etc., in all parts of the city, everyday.

He quickly approached us and with barely a greeting launched into an intense description of being inside Tower One when Tower Two collapsed. He imitated the sensation of what it was like in the building by violently shaking his whole body. He described seeing Father Judge just as the building began to fall and yelled to him not to go out a door to the outside. He had also seen Assistant Chief Gerard Barbara when the chief first arrived at the scene. According to Ritchie, who had been on an elevated portion of the Trade Center Plaza, Chief Barbara looked up at the buildings and then at him and simply said, "This is bad, Ritchie, this is bad."

He also spoke of taking pictures of the plaza through the blood-splattered lobby windows of Tower One while people jumped to their deaths. Somehow, while in the process of escaping, Ritchie ended up in, or on, an outdoor balcony of Building Six, where he fell and lost six rolls of film he had taken, or his camera. Those rolls were lost, but I recently heard that either they or Ritchie's camera were recovered.

Ritchie went on almost nonstop in a hyper state. Concerned about his well being, I interrupted him and told him that he should go and speak to someone from the Counseling Unit. He answered rapidly that he was all right. I turned to the priest looking for some back-up and said, "Father, tell him he's got to go talk to the Counseling Unit." My attention was drawn away by someone else but I could hear the priest speaking directly to Ritchie, "Well, it's good that you are talking about it…." That was all I heard.

Ritchie insisted on taking my picture. I stood with my back to the mountain of wreckage. It looks as if it is right behind me and deceptively small in the photo. Actually, it was a good distance away across a chasm. A twenty-foot portable ladder against the pile brings the mound into proper perspective.

Afterwards we all entered a loading bay on the west side of Building Six to show the priest a cross formed by broken steel beams in the center of the building. I believe firefighter Tom Lynch had pointed this out to me earlier.

The steel cross has become an iconic figure of September 11. It was recovered and mounted for a while on a pedestal on the east side of the site. Since then it has been moved to Saint Peter's Catholic Church, a block north.

People are fascinated by this almost miraculous symbol rising out of the wreckage. Of course, there are always nay-sayers, and rumors quickly circulated that construction workers assembled the cross out of steel from the wreckage. This obviously is not the case. I saw the cross in the ruins of Building Six and have a photo of it there.

I found out from the priest before we parted that he was not from the NYPD but from California's Newport Beach Police Department. He had come three thousand miles east to help.

PSYCHOLOGICAL HELP

Something was eating at me as we were leaving the site on Thursday afternoon, walking north toward the buses. We still had not been given any real assignment in the recovery effort yet. That bothered me, but there was something else. I was concerned whether or not I would be able to handle actual victim recovery. The feeling came not so much out of fear or revulsion but from a feeling of empathy for the innocents murdered in such a brutal way.

These thoughts were with me as we stopped for some bottled water and snacks at a stand set up outside the Manhattan Community College campus. Someone must have been reading my mind because a woman stepped over, greeted us, and explained that she was a psychiatrist (maybe a psychologist). She asked if we were doing all right and if any of us needed to talk about anything.

After a moment of hesitation I asked if I could speak to her for a moment. We stepped away from the others and I explained what had been going through my mind. I don't remember what she actually said but it had a calming effect. I also told her about my desire to write something about my experiences there and how I was conflicted about that, too. She gave me reassurances on that matter also.

I felt better after speaking to her. She must have been happy that someone availed himself of her services because she gave me a hug and a Hershey bar, still a valuable commodity at that time and place.

I didn't know her name at the time but later saw a newspaper article about her services at Ground Zero.

THE LAST NIGHT

There was a flurry of activity on the rubble pile on the night of Friday, September 28. A peak of wreckage had formed around the area of one of the stairwells of the north tower. A group of firefighters worked intently at the top of the pile. Although I was at a distance I recognized one as Battalion Chief John Salka, who had been back and forth at the command post a number of times. I knew Chief Salka by name and reputation, which was excellent. I attended some classes he had given at various firefighter training programs. His dry sense of humor was a source of laughter at these classes. I remember him describing the intense heat of a bad fire at the Empire State Building years before. He stated facetiously that, "...even the hoses were on fire!"

Later, describing the increase of heat as they moved toward the seat of the blaze, he said, "... the *insides* of the hoses were on fire!"[28]

As I watched the searchers from a distance, word began to spread that someone had been found. A short time later Chief Salka returned to the command post, where he explained some action he had taken to the deputy chief, who outranked him, there. I got the impression that he had made known the identity of the firefighter who had been found without waiting for forensic verification and/or official authority. I heard him say something like, "Hey chief, when I look on the coat and it says 'Hatton,' and I look in the pocket and it says 'Hatton,' it's Terry Hatton!"

Terry was not removed immediately. The department had a tradition that a fallen member be recovered by his own company whenever possible. Terry's Rescue 1 was summoned from its quarters on West 43rd Street. They arrived after a few minutes, left their rig, and began the sad climb to the top of the rubble pile.

Battalion Chief Jack Pritchard stood nearby. I did not know him personally but I knew him by reputation and from seeing his photos. At the time he was one of only two firefighters to have earned the FDNY's highest honor, the James Gordon Bennett Medal, twice. He walked over to me and directed me to get some members assembled for an honor guard.

A handful of 308 guys sat on the street nearby, along with two volunteer firefighters from Long Island. The latter must have been there on their own, since outside participation in the recovery, except for specialists, had ended.

My first instinct was to just have my guys form the honor guard, but then I looked at the vollies sitting there.

They were there because they wanted to be, and they were not getting paid to do so. I said to them, "Hey fellas, could you give us a hand?" They were happy to do so and I was glad I asked them.

I had everyone line up facing north on Vesey St., just to the west of West St. Firefighters, in some formations I had seen, had been removing their helmets when the honored dead passed by. I told everyone to leave their helmets on because we would be doing a salute. I would call them to attention at the appropriate time.

I'm not sure why I had them line up there. It had something to do with where the ambulance which would transport Terry was parked. Since the guys from Rescue would be approaching us from the south, our rear, I turned around and waited.

I have described earlier about my inability, or unwillingness, to recognize certain things. I knew exactly what I should be looking for. I saw them approach but, as in earlier cases, I simply had trouble registering what I was seeing. I had to actually tell myself that the big guys from Rescue carrying the Stokes was what I was supposed to be looking for.

They were almost to me when I turned and called "Attention!" The procession came up on my right and turned left in front of us. I called "Hand salute!" The guys forming the honor guard stood to my left. Chief Pritchard faced me from across the street. We held our salute until Terry and his men were well past us. I called "To!" and we stood down.

Later, Engine 308 stood on the west side again in some kind of stand-by mode. By this time a bridge had been constructed across a chasm, connecting West Street with the rubble pile. Firefighters worked at the top of the pile.

A few came down with buckets of material and began examining it. We joined them and saw that some of the material they had was pieces of a firefighter's bunker coat. There was also a bundle of a light steel frame with pieces of a heavy plastic box attached. At first we did not know what we had, but then realized it was the frame and regulator of a Scott 4.5 self contained breathing apparatus—a firefighter's "mask."

We examined the material closely, hoping to find some way of identifying the firefighter to whom it belonged. While we were doing this, Joe Gick said that he was going up on the pile. I told him to go ahead and I would be right there too. He and the other guys from 308 headed up.

I gave the material a final look. There were no identifying marks on any of it. I started the climb up the rubble pile. I reached the top where 308 had begun searching with other firefighters. No sooner had I reached the top than a siren sounded, announcing that the pile had to be cleared of searchers since heavy equipment was about to be used. Someone or something just did not want me, or us, that involved.

We reluctantly climbed down with the others. After a while our tour was completed. I never got back. I always thought that I would be assigned again, but I never was.

THE PUBLIC

The task force assignment came to an end, as did the month of September, 2001. The department returned to its normal working chart and I, through mutual exchanges of tours with Lt. Bob Urso, resumed working twenty-four hours on and seventy-two hours off.

Life became a weird dance between the pre-and post-9/11 worlds. Daughter Katie attended school, played little league soccer on weekends, and took Irish step dance lessons on Monday evenings. Kelly still taught in Katie's school, ran PTA meetings, and attended functions such as "Meet your teachers night."

I went back and forth to work at Engine 308. The company responded to alarms, fought fires, inspected buildings, drilled, prepared meals, and dealt with a suddenly interested public on an almost celebrity level. We also listened to four-5-signals in the normal course of firehouse duties and waited for word about Terry McShane.

The firehouse had more outside traffic then it ever had before. The shrine out front grew with things like candles and flowers added by neighbors. People came by with food, supplies, tools, work gloves, clothing, and other items they felt could be used at Ground Zero. Boxes of donated items accumulated on the apparatus floor behind the rig.

One elderly lady came to quarters with a couple of packages of white T-shirts. One proby, who met her at the open apparatus door, told her that we really couldn't use something like that. I had just come downstairs as she turned away dejectedly and heard her say she would just take them back with her. I asked him what had happened. When he explained I had him bring the woman back. We apologized, accepted her donation, and thanked her. The people needed to help, and they had to have the feeling that they were helping.

The firefighters' families pitched in when they could, too. Tom Lynch's wife, a massage therapist by profession, came in to give back massages to the guys, setting up her table on the apparatus floor. I was the last to try this. Mrs.

Lynch said, not surprisingly, that I was the worst, meaning most tense, of the whole company.

Some wanted to help in other ways. A local artist came by, or was invited by one of the guys. He wanted to paint some kind of symbolic work on the outside of the apparatus door. I think firefighter Tony Bonfiglio sought my okay. I said yes, believing that the painting would be on one, but no more than four panels of the door. I came in on a later day to find the whole door covered in an elaborate blue mural.

We also had spontaneous visitors, due to all of the outpouring of feeling for the FDNY in the aftermath. A few of us stood outside the open door of the firehouse one day when a car pulled up. A young Italian-looking guy, dripping in gold and slathered in cologne hopped out. He gave me a big hug, said he was up from Florida, and just wanted to say hello. He stood there with us for a few minutes, just smiling, and then he left.

One evening I was sitting in the engine office, trying to get some paperwork done when I was summoned to the apparatus floor. I found the guys gathered there with a short, very serious-looking civilian. He said he had prepared a song for us and he had been going around to all firehouses singing it. He broke out a cassette tape player, fired it up and launched into his song, his face knitted in loving sincerity.

I don't remember most of the song but its main lyric was, "*You're not alone, you're not alo-alo-alone.*" The man's heart was in the right place but I'm pretty sure he did not land any recording contracts afterwards.

This came at a time when everyone's emotions were on razor's edge. The slightest thing could induce a fight, reduce one to blubbering tears, or bring on mad-house laughter. It took all of my self control not to make eye contact with any of the other guys. An uncomfortable silence followed the performance. Randy Rodrigues came to the rescue. "Awesome, man!" was all he said.

Our visitor left. I think I directed him to Engine 303, where I believed Gary Velilla was working. I returned to the office resolving not to come downstairs again unless the firehouse itself was on fire.

A group of neighbors provided the most memorable visit. I was summoned to the apparatus floor again one evening. A group of men, women, and children from our South Ozone Park/Richmond Hill neighborhood had come by. The leader asked if it would be all right to hold a Hindu prayer service at our shrine out front. Of course it was. The guys from 308 stood just inside the apparatus doors, while the neighbors assembled out front. They conducted a very beautiful service, not one word of it in English. Their prayers had a sonorous, chanting quality to them. The whole effect was very soothing, as was the sincere concern of the people involved.

They concluded their ceremony and the leader caught me a bit by surprise by stepping over and asking me to say a few words. A couple of the 308 guys looked at me. Kevin Crosby smiled as if to say, "Now what are you going to do?"

I shook myself out of the almost meditative state brought on by the service and thanked all of them. I explained that although we, the firefighters, did not understand the words there was a quality of the prayers as coming from the heart that transcended language barriers. I also made some comments about how we are all Americans, and that the current tragedy has brought us all closer. Finally, I invited them all in for a look at the rigs and firefighting equipment. I asked the guys to show them around, open up the soda machine for the kids, and offer tea or coffee to any of the adults. It was a very good, peaceful time, uninterrupted by any alarms.

CAPTAIN TERENCE HATTON, RESCUE 1

Searchers found Terry Hatton on September 28. His funeral was held at Saint Patrick's Cathedral on October 4. I donned my dress uniform and took the A-train into Manhattan. I may have taken the train from my old neighborhood of Howard Beach, or I may have gone to the firehouse and taken the A-train spur where it terminates at Liberty Ave. and Lefferts Blvd. I do not remember that but I do remember that when I got on the train, in uniform, I felt that all eyes were upon me. I tried to minimize myself by standing in a corner and facing the wall of the subway car. A woman standing nearby asked me with genuine concern if I was all right. I thanked her and told her that I was.

The train arrived at its stop beneath the streets of Manhattan at 53rd Street and Fifth Avenue, two blocks north of the cathedral. Two non-FDNY firefighters stepped from another subway car. They appeared lost so I gave them directions to street level. I walked slowly as I exited the subway. Another woman stopped on her entry into the system, put her hand on my arm and asked if I was okay. I assured her that I was.

Thousands lined Fifth Ave, outside of Saint Patrick's. I ended up in the front row of firefighters and fire officers facing, and slightly to the right of, the cathedral doors.

The funeral procession arrived, coming from our left. I heard the bagpipers before they arrived in my line of sight. I was surprised to see only two of them—one from the Fire Department and one from the Police Department. Normally the Fire Department's Pipe and Drum Band's presence at department funerals may be as many as fifty men. It hit me that all the other pipers and drummers from both departments were either working at Ground Zero, spread thin at other fire and police funerals, or, as in the case of some Fire Department band members, missing in the Trade Center wreckage.

I felt it a shame that a fire officer of Terry's stature should only have two pipers at his funeral. Then I thought of how ridiculous that was because the real sadness lay in the fact that we were at his funeral in the first place.

Earlier I mentioned what I felt to be an inaccuracy in Dennis Smith's *Report From Ground Zero*, and it involves the pipers at this funeral. Dennis wrote, "The Emerald Society Pipes & Drums are here in almost full force, more than fifty of them…"[29]

When I read this in 2002 I thought back to the funeral and what I saw with my own eyes. Because I read contradictory information from this book, I actually began to doubt what I had observed. This proves nothing except to reinforce one of my long-standing beliefs about the power of the printed word.

Terry's family, friends, and co-workers rapidly filled the cathedral. I said hello and chatted a bit just inside the doors with Jack Lerch, fire buff extraordinaire and longtime friend of the FDNY. Jack is active in a number of Fire Department related organizations, and volunteers his time at the Fire Department's Mand Library at the Division of Training. He is a walking encyclopedia of FDNY history and lore. He, of course, was as much affected by the department's losses as anyone on the job.

I took a seat in a pew toward the rear and tried to lose myself in the granite magnificence of Saint Pat's. A number of people came to the altar to eulogize Terry during the service. One was Mayor Giuliani. His assistant, Beth Petrone, was Terry's wife. Tim Brown, who had worked with Terry in Rescue, but was now attached to the Office of Emergency Management, also said some words. He spoke of Terry's considerable firefighting skills, and how Terry had only two words for critiquing the performance of his men at fires. Their actions were either "Outstanding" or "Unacceptable," and Terry would only stand for the former. Tim got some laughs and caused some squirming among the chiefs in the front rows when he spoke of Terry bending the rules a bit. He described with admiration Terry's habit of wearing a short dungaree jacket instead of his assigned and required bunker coat at some fires, but then caught himself and added "I know the chiefs don't like to hear this."

Finally he related his experience of meeting Terry for the last time just outside of Tower One on September 11. Terry came over to him, hugged him, and bade him a final farewell. The way I remember the story from the funeral is that Terry said, "My brother, I'm afraid we're all going to die here today." Later, Tim gave official testimony on his actions to the FDNY's Safety Command. In it he related Terry's words as "I love you, brother. It might be the last time I see you." [30]

Has my memory of the words failed me or were they changed to soften their impact? I could be wrong about what was actually said. Whatever Terry's thoughts were at the time he definitely knew the seriousness of the situation, and he still went toward the danger in order to do his job.

Terry's father, retired Deputy Chief Kenneth Hatton, also spoke. At the end of his eulogy he invited everyone to stand and give a round of applause for Captain Terence Hatton of the FDNY. Saint Patrick's thundered.

Afterwards, out front, I spoke briefly to Commissioner Von Essen. It was the first time I had seen him since the attack. His family was with him and he posed for a picture holding his granddaughter on the steps of the cathedral.

A female reporter approached me to get a statement about Terry. I told her the story of last seeing him a year earlier after the battalion chief's exam and how I had to look up at him even though he was standing in the street and I was on the curb. The reporter defined my description very succinctly. She said "So, it was as if he was getting taller as you looked at him." Amen.

I do not remember anything of the subway ride home or what I did for the rest of the day. I worked that night and the following day, Friday, October 5, in Engine 308.

CELEBRITIES II

Everyone reached for some kind of normalcy amid the chaos and stress. Kelly, Katie, and I went on our annual Columbus Day excursion to the Bronx Zoo on October 8. It was a family tradition we had been following for years. It was always a welcome break to drive to the Bronx and lose ourselves in the maze of paths at the famous zoo. This year it was more important than ever. However, as with everything else, an underlying guilt at being able to enjoy it came with the fun and peace.

The entertainment community, still doing its part in the only way it could, was heard again on October 20. Paul McCartney organized a giant rock gala at Madison Square Garden for the benefit and entertainment of emergency service workers and victims' families.

McCartney did an outstanding job of assembling an amazing roster of the biggest names in music, film, comedy, and politics for the show. I believe Mayor Giuliani favored the idea since it would show that New York City would not cave in to terrorism. However, many in the Fire Department and elsewhere felt that it was a case of too much too soon.

I reluctantly tuned in to the live TV broadcast. There were many uniformed emergency service personnel in the audience. The part I saw was very loud and raucous. A number of uniformed people danced on and off the stage with whatever band was playing at the time. I think it was Mick Jagger and Keith Richards from the Rolling Stones. It seemed to me that there were a large number of Emergency Medical Service people. It gave me the impression of forced gaiety—all a little too much hard partying. I didn't watch for too long.

One notable non-entertainment part of the show was the appearance on stage of firefighter Mike Moran, of Rockaway, NY. Mike's brother, Battalion Chief John Moran, had been killed on September 11. Mike directed a comment to his brother's murderer, "In the true spirit of the Irish people, Osama bin Laden, you can kiss my royal Irish ass!" The audience roared its approval. The newspapers and media loved it. Others wondered what the ramifications would be.

FLIGHT 587

I worked the day tour of November 12 and was in the engine office when Jimmy Ferretti's voice, with a definite edge to it, came over the intercom, "Battalion's going to Rockaway!"

Rockaway is a barrier-island type peninsula running across the south side of the borough of Queens, just as the Jones Beach area runs along the south side of Nassau County. It is a thin but highly populated strip of land between Jamaica Bay and the Atlantic Ocean.

Rockaway, at its closest point to us, was about ten miles away. It was not unheard of for the Battalion to travel that far on a response, but it had to be some unique situation—a big multiple alarm, or a number of smaller, separate fires each requiring the response of a Battalion Chief. The announcement of the Battalion's run puzzled me since I had not heard anything over the voice alarm regarding anything big happening in Rockaway.

I came down the stairs as the Battalion Chief and his aide were turning out. I asked one of my guys what was happening in Rockaway. He replied something like, "Are you kidding? Didn't you hear over the voice alarm that there was a plane crash in Rockaway?"

It was American Airlines Flight 587, which crashed in the Rockaway neighborhood of Belle Harbor. It killed all 260 people on board and five on the ground.

I never heard anything over the voice alarm. Or, did I hear it and completely block it out? I don't know. However, Rockaway—the home of Mike Moran, who had recently told Osama bin Laden to kiss his ass—was now the scene of another jet liner crash. Everyone's thoughts went in the same direction with this one. Terrorism was later ruled out by the National Transportation Safety Board, but there are still questions in some circles.

I went back upstairs, then climbed a ladder to the roof. I could see on the horizon to the south a now too familiar sight—a roiling black cloud coming from one of the neighborhoods on the peninsula. I returned to the apparatus floor, where the guys gathered around the department radio. If the battalion could go, we could go. And everyone wanted to go.

Finally an alarm came in. Someone announced that we were going to Rockaway. The guys scrambled to turn out. I looked at the computer printout for our box (alarm location) and realized that we were going to Rockaway all right, but not to the plane crash. We were responding to a water flow alarm at a nursing home a mile or two east of the plane crash. All the companies in Rockaway had either been assigned to the crash or were operating elsewhere. Units off the peninsula, like 308, were being dispatched there to handle emergencies and other fire duty.

We responded south on Crossbay Boulevard, over the North Channel Bridge, through the neighborhood of Broad Channel, and over the Rockaway Beach Bridge. I kept my eyes on the ominous black cloud the whole way in. It was, once again, an unnervingly familiar sight.

We crossed the bridge into Rockaway, turned east and drove a few blocks to the nursing home. A surge in water pressure in the home's sprinkler system caused the water flow alarm to sound. The system then reset itself. There was no fire and no danger. These types of alarms were fairly common.

I noticed something familiar about the nursing home and its location. I realized that it had been the old Rockaway Beach Hospital where I had been born forty-nine years earlier. I had not been down that way in a long while and never knew the abandoned hospital had been turned into a nursing home.

I went "10-8" on the computer in the rig, notifying the dispatcher that Engine 308 was in service and available on the air. I also contacted him via the department radio, informing him that we were close to, and in sight of, the plane crash, and asked if he wanted us to respond there. He replied that 308 should remain "10-8."

I was not happy about this. Technically we should have returned to the firehouse or at least our own response area then. I had Jimmy Ferretti park the rig at the curb in front of a McDonald's on Beach Channel Drive. We stayed on the air and listened to the action at the crash over the radio and our handi-talkies. We watched as other units responded over the Rockaway Beach Bridge to the crash while we sat there. I may have gotten on the horn again to nudge the dispatcher a bit, but to no avail. The guys stood on the sidewalk, looking west toward the smoke. I sat in the cab monitoring the radio.

Tom Lynch, giving voice to everyone's frustration, said to me, "Why don't we just go down there?" I couldn't do that. I couldn't commit the company to an operation without being assigned. We would still have been recorded as an available unit but we would not have been actually available if needed for any other fires or emergencies.

We sat there for maybe twenty minutes to a half-hour, watching and listening until we received another alarm. Engine 308 traveled the long way back to our own response area to extinguish a small outdoor rubbish fire.

This, the situation on September 11 of waiting at the command post for hours and in the later week of being constantly held in reserve so many times were taking their toll on all of us. Looking back on it I am reminded of a line from the John Ford film *They Were Expendable.* The admiral tells the young PT boat commander, anxious to get into the action against the Japanese Navy, "Look, Brick, when the manager says 'sacrifice' you lay down a bunt and let the other fellow hit the home run." But that didn't help us then, and it still bothers me today.

FIREFIGHTER TERENCE MCSHANE, ENGINE 308

Once again I sat at the desk in the engine office one night when the phone rang. The house watchman announced over the intercom, "Cap, department phone." It was the captain of Ladder 101, to which Terry McShane had been detailed. He said that it looked like searchers had found Terry. He gave me what details he had, which were not too many.

The question came up as to which company, Engine 308 or ladder 101, would be handling the funeral. Terry was officially assigned to 308, but he was detailed to and working with 101 on September 11. I thought Ladder 101 would have its hands full since it had lost several members. However, it was explained to me that they would be the company of record for the funeral. I offered 308's help in anything that needed to be done. I went downstairs to let the guys know. It seemed that some of them had already heard some word of Terry being found.

Details of this part of the 9/11 saga remain more muddled for me than others. Maybe it was my closeness to the whole thing. Maybe things were just adding up collectively. For example, at one point a group of people from the firehouse and their wives planned to go out and visit Terry's wife, Cathy. I have no memory of whether this happened before or after he was found. Kelly and I drove out to West Islip on Long Island, where their house was under construction. Despite the address and detailed directions of where the McShanes were living while the house was being built, I never was able to locate the house. We drove around for about an hour before conceding defeat. It still bothers me today since I cannot say why I could not find the house. Did I have bad information or was I psychologically blocking myself from finding it? I truly do not know.

Terry was waked at Overlook Beach, along the Robert Moses Causeway, miles east of Jones Beach. He had been a lifeguard there years before and had met Cathy at Overlook. There is a pavilion-type building there but I think the wake itself was held in a large tent.

I met the guys from 308 there and saw many others I knew from the job. We greeted Cathy to express our condolences. I could barely choke out my words. She seemed very brave and strong under the circumstances. Later I approached her to have a few private words. I stood behind her and opened my mouth to speak but no words came out. It was if a hand gripped my throat. I could not utter a sound. I stood there foolishly for a few seconds and then moved away.

One of the people I met at the wake was retired Battalion Chief Gabe Abbinanti. Gabe had been my first captain when I was assigned to Engine 332, in 1977. He was a great firefighter and fire officer. I had not seen him in a long time so we spoke for a while.

Firefighters, at the time I came on the job, were given a "1620" key. This key opened the door to any firehouse in the city in the days before combination locks. In addition, they opened most of the alarm boxes, in order to rewind the alarm, and had several other uses. Engine 332 did not have any extra ones when I was assigned, so Captain Abbinanti gave me his. I reminded him of this during our conversation, removed my key chain from my pocket, and showed him the key that he had given me twenty-four years earlier. He had scratched his initials "G.A." onto it; however, time and use had worn it down so that the initials looked like "L.A." I told him I would send it back to him after I retired in the coming year. He told me he wanted me to keep it. I still have it today.

I stood with a group of guys from 308 outside the tent. Everyone was pretty tense and somber. I felt very detached and not able to join in their conversation as I normally would have with a group of firefighters. I drifted down to the shoreline where a few people had gathered before sunset. I stood alone and did not take the usual comfort from the ocean that I would have.

Terry McShane's funeral was held the following day on Long Island. Kelly and I drove out early and were there before most of the people assembled. I waited on the steps of the church as the Fire Department's Ceremonial Unit arrived.

The Ceremonial Unit is manned by light-duty firefighters assigned to the Division of Training. They direct the proper procedures for Department funerals and other official events. The lieutenant in charge of McShane's funeral had been a young firefighter who worked with my father years before. I knew him but not well.

The lieutenant and I walked through the church to see how things would be set up. Of course, there was a center aisle and there may have been an aisle separating the church pews into front and rear sections. It was either on this aisle or in the rear I noticed two small tables, about waist high and painted gold. I assumed they were used for holding chalices of bread and wine for those receiving Communion in the rear of the church.

We went back outside to the steps to plan things and await the arrival of the Captain and members of Ladder 101, Engine 202, which shared quarters with 101, and Engine 308.

Things did not proceed smoothly. I thought that by this time and under these sad circumstances of so many funerals that the Ceremonial Unit would have had things down to a science. Every point had to be decided. It went like this. The Ceremonial lieutenant and his men debated the options, let's say "A, B, or C" of how each step of the procession to and entry into the church should be handled, without reaching a decision. Then, they turned to me and asked, "What do you think, Cap?" I listened to their options on every point, weighed the possibilities, and told them "Go with option B," and explained my reasons. They nodded their heads in agreement until another member of their unit approached saying something like, "Okay, let's do the step according to plan "A," and they would start all over again. After this happened several times I felt the PTSD temper begin to rear its ugly head and I had to detach myself from the planning stage.

Finally everyone arrived and we awaited a volunteer engine apparatus which would carry Terry's casket to the church steps. It was decided that I and the captain of Ladder 101 would march in front of the rig, slightly to the right and left of the respective headlights. A detail of guys from each company would march alongside the engine and act as pall bearers. The rig would stop in front of the church and at a given signal, both captains would do an "about-face" and join the firefighters at the rear. We would then carry the casket into the church and place it in front of the altar before the large group of mourners entered. I missed my cue when the rig stopped in front of the church, so things came off with a bit less than Arlington Cemetery efficiency, but there was another problem.

The guys had carried the casket into the church when the lieutenant from the Ceremonial Unit pointed out that the undertaker had forgotten to bring the wheeled carriage that the casket normally rests upon in front of the altar. He added something like, "I guess we'll just have to put it on the floor."

I came close to blowing up then. "We're not putting Terry on the floor!" I said, "I don't care if we have to all take turns holding the casket the whole time, but we're not putting him on the floor!"

I started to devise a system of relief where eight of us would hold the casket and be replaced by others every ten minutes of so. Then I remembered the two tables I had seen earlier.

I located them again. They were of a very sturdy metal and not wood. I tested one by leaning my full weight on it. I got some help and we carried them to the front of the church. We positioned them, and they made a perfect platform.

I sat on the far right side of the church toward the front, with members of Engine 308. There were many members of both the Fire and Police Departments present. The Mass and eulogies have faded into a blur by now. I think it was one of Terry's older brothers who described Terry's enthusiasm for playing rugby with them, even though he was much smaller than they. A firefighter from Engine 202 spoke of seeing Terry for the last time as

Ladder 101 left their quarters for the Trade Center. The firefighter had run out of their firehouse with one last bit of information from the dispatcher while Ladder 101 was still on the apron. "They're reporting thirty floors of fire!" he announced. He then described the look of excitement and determination to go on Terry's face.

I had been asked to prepare a short eulogy for Terry. I wrote one but I knew that I would never be able to deliver it. I had asked Lieutenant Joe Mills if he would be able to. He stepped up to the task and I gave him a copy a few days earlier. He read the eulogy in a low, emotion-muffled voice. He did a good job.

The church had two sections of pews on either side of the altar and facing the altar. The wives from Engine 308 and from the other companies sat directly in front of us. Kelly and the other women dabbed at their eyes with tissues rolled up to the size of marbles. I realized that she and probably the others had never been to a line-of-duty funeral before.

The service ended, we left the church, and lined the steps. The pallbearers carried Terry's casket past us and placed it on the fire apparatus. Cathy McShane and her sons came out and waited on the steps. I had one last task to perform.

It was my duty to present the McShane children, seven-year-old Aidan and four-year-old twins Colin and Sean, with replicas of their father's fire helmet. I did so, saying some words about how their father wore the helmet in protection of the people of the City of New York. I managed to choke out the words. I do not know how I did it but I did. This final gesture left me weak and shaken.

We stood at attention and saluted Firefighter Terrance McShane a final time as the apparatus pulled away. I do not remember anything about the bagpipes and drums, although I know they were there.

There was some kind of collation after the cemetery. I could not bring myself to attend.

NOVEMBER INTO DECEMBER, 2001

Somehow we celebrated Thanksgiving, on November 22, and Kelly's birthday three days later. Things were not all that festive in either case. November gave way to December. I was assigned to terrorism training on December 10—not to become a terrorist but how to be aware of and respond to terrorist attacks.

Somehow Engine 308 held its annual Christmas party in a hall on Long Island. It was a subdued party, held mostly for the many children of 308's firefighters. We attended and brought along Katie's best friend Megan Auwarter. Santa arrived and gave out gifts for the kids.

Cathy McShane and her boys attended. Once again I walked up behind her to speak to her. Once again the hand gripped my throat, and no words came out.

We left the party and drove to Jones Beach. The West End section of the causeway was brightly lighted with Christmas decorations—large frames in various holiday shapes, illuminated by tens of thousands of colorful lights. We entered the line of cars, drove through the display, and listened to Christmas song and carols. We stopped for a while at the Theodore Roosevelt Nature Center on the beach, a small museum/aquarium displaying the flora and fauna of the Jones Beach area. The center was brightly lighted. Adults and children moved about, looking with interest at the various displays. The night outside the large windows and warmth of the building was very black and cold.

I had my first of several World Trade Center medical exams at the Fire Department's Bureau of Health Services on December 22. The program is designed to monitor the physical, mental, and emotional health of those firefighters who operated at the Trade Center. I have returned a number of times over the years for follow-up exams.

I went on annual leave (vacation) from December 16 to 25. Somehow we celebrated Christmas, which fell that year on a Tuesday, exactly fifteen weeks to the day after September 11. I worked my last set of tours for 2001, a night tour and then the following day on December 27 into the twenty-eighth.

We wished one another "Happy New Year" at midnight on December 31. We wished it for ourselves, our country, our city, and the FDNY. After the Father's Day fire, the crash of Flight 587, and especially the World Trade Center, the Pentagon, and Flight 93, 2002 had to be so.

EPILOGUE

I sat in the *Thank God Its Friday* restaurant of the Radisson Hotel in Austin, Texas, on February 28, 2002. My friend, Professor Paul Andrew Hutton, had organized an extensive exhibition on the life, legend, and impact on popular culture of American frontiersman, David Crockett, at the new Bob Bullock Texas History Museum. He invited me to be on a panel for the event, along with other Crockett and Western historians, William R. Chemerka, William B. Davis, Michael A. Lofaro, and Paul Fees.

The panel was scheduled for later that day. I had been there the night before at a reception for the exhibition. Fess Parker, television's quintessential Davy Crockett of the 1950s, was also on hand. He graciously greeted a long line of admirers for autographs, photos, and a few words with each. I had met him a couple of times before and had corresponded with him over the years.

I waited my turn, until almost everyone else was through. I got on line with a program of the event I wanted him to sign. I also planned on thanking him for getting me interested in Davy Crockett back in the '50s, which led to my interest in history and eventually writing. He was my hero and greatest childhood adult figure influence, second only to Fireman William F. Groneman, Jr., of Ladder Company 6.

I finally made it to the table where he was seated. I handed him the program, which he signed, and I opened my mouth to speak. Before I could say anything Fess said, "Bill, I want to thank you for all you have done for us." I was so surprised that I didn't even get a chance to thank him. The line moved on and that was it. At first I thought he had thanked me for the things I had written setting the historical record straight about Davy Crockett. Later I realized that he was thanking, through me, the Fire Department of the City of New York for its actions on September 11, 2001.

I thought about this and about what I would say at the symposium as I sat alone in the restaurant waiting for breakfast. I fidgeted nervously, checking my watch every few minutes. My waitress walked by as the time read 7:59 plus. I called her over, showed her the numbers on the watch, and said, "Miss, do you see what time it is?" She looked annoyed and somewhat angry because she assumed I was complaining about the speed of service of my breakfast. The time turned 8:00 a.m. I said, "It's exactly eight o'clock. That means it is 9:00 a.m. in New York City, and right now at 9:00 a.m. I am officially retired from the New York City Fire Department."

She looked at my blue sweat shirt with "FDNY" and "Engine 308" emblazoned on the back and a Maltese cross on the left breast, and she teared up. "Oh my God," she said in a weak voice, "I'm going to cry!" I felt like crying myself. She left to bring my breakfast. I tipped her more than the breakfast cost for being with me when I retired.

And that is how I left the service of the Fire Department of the City of New York—in the *TGIF* in the Radisson Hotel, on the Colorado River, in Austin, capital of the Lone Star State of Texas, on February 28, 2002.

I returned to Ground Zero for the official closing ceremonies at the World Trade Center site on May 30th . I met my brother, Michael, downtown, and we stood with a bunch of guys from 308 as a final piece of steel beam was removed from the pit. We gave a "hand salute" yards away from where we rendered one for Terry Hatton, eight months earlier.

Kelly, Katie, and I moved to Texas three months later. We moved away from family, friends, New York City, Long Island, Jones Beach, the FDNY, and Ground Zero. It was a great deal of things to have happened in the span of one year.

I returned to New York one month after our move for the first anniversary of September 11. I got downtown only minutes before the ceremony began. Tens of thousands of people were already crowding the streets around the site. I approached from Broadway and tried to gain access to the World Trade Center grounds via Cortland Street, where Engine 308 had relieved the Brooklyn engine company one year before. Even though I was in full uniform, I was stopped by a young, female police officer who told me that I could not go down that street because there were too many people there already. I wondered where she had been one year earlier.

Rather than argue, I resignedly went back to Broadway and found another way to Church Street and the site. I stood with Matt Swan and other firefighters as the names of the 9/11 victims were read. At 8:46 a.m., a year to the minute of the first plane slamming into Tower One, the wind suddenly kicked up, raising a cloud of World Trade Center dust over the Ground Zero crater.

I returned again a month later for an FDNY memorial service held at Madison Square Garden. I sat with the boys from 308. Already there were some new faces in the company. I asked a proby if he would mind moving down one seat so I could sit and chat with Wayne Slater.

Officials sat on the stage below us and to our left. Families of Fire Department victims sat in chairs on the main floor facing the stage. A string quartet played classical, patriotic, and Irish tunes as the names of the 343 lost Fire Department members were read. A variety of images of each person appeared on large screens. Ronan Tynan was there and sang "God Bless America." I sobbed and could not control the tears during the roll call of names. I sensed the proby to my left glancing at me. I thought to myself that he had a long way to go before understanding why, but I knew he would some day.

I also attended a ceremony at Engine 308, dedicating memorial plaques to Terry McShane and Ronnie Gies. I still was not able to speak to Cathy McShane.

I have been back and forth to New York City a number of times over the past ten years. I've tried to make a visit to Ground Zero every time. I was not successful in that during my last trip in November, 2010, having never even made it into Manhattan that time. However, I did recreate my long walk at Jones Beach of September 11, 2001.

AFTERWORD

This has been a personal record of what I remember happening on September 11, 2001, and during the months following. If there are discrepancies with the official record of events, and/or anyone else's recollections, it is strictly due to the "faulty, warpy reservoir of memory," my own and others'.

Some have said that we need to move on from 9/11. It is in the past and should stay there. Many have moved on already. More than once a person has said to me things like, "September 11, now what year was that again?" I know that some years down the line, the date and event will become like Pearl Harbor or the Kennedy assassination, mentioned in a two-inch column on page eight of some newspaper.

Luckily others, like the United States Navy SEALs, have not moved on yet. During the writing of the final pages of this memoir a SEAL team, supported by other elite elements of the U.S. military, raided a compound in Pakistan and killed Osama bin Laden, the homicidal mastermind of the 9/11 attacks. Appropriately he died like a dog, and now pollutes the Arabian Sea. Thank you, Navy SEALs, and all the unsung military heroes involved in that operation.

It is difficult for people, civilian, military, emergency service workers, who were there at the Pentagon or World Trade Center, or for families and loved ones of victims, including those on Flight 93, to move on.

Speaking personally, there has not been a day since September 11, 2001, that I have not thought back to some aspect of it. I do not wake up in the morning obsessing over it but there is always some stimulus: photos, TV shows, books, references to the FDNY, or New York City, etc., which always brings me back. For some reason I always seem to glance at a digital clock when it is 9:11 a.m. and 9:11 p.m. every day. I imagine it is considerably worse for those more tragically affected than I had been.

Thinking back I know I could have, and should have, done more in many ways. I often miss a pre-9/11 world, incorrectly perceived as innocent and free of cares. We can't go back and change things—things that happened, things we did, or did not do. We can only move forward and live life to the fullest and as best we can.

However, every now and then…

It's 8:30 on a warm, late summer morning on Long Island. I feel great. I stretch out, take my water bottle, and start reciting my Rosary. I leave the parking lot of Field Six and head west on the boardwalk. It is the beginning of one beautiful day at Jones Beach…

RECOMMENDED READING, VIEWING, AND LISTENING

Many books and articles have been written and documentaries made about September 11, 2001. The following are a few that I highly recommend for a greater understanding of the New York City Fire Department's role that day, or for a background of the FDNY itself.

ARTICLES

Brown, Larry. "The Special Breed—You eat together, you sleep together, and you die together." *Men's Journal*. (November 2001): 84.

Court, Ben, Josh Dean, Sean Flynn, Tom Foster, Devin Friedman, Alex Markels, Michael Rey, and David Willey. "The Fire Fighters—When the unthinkable happened they got the call. The harrowing stories of New York City's Bravest." *Men's Journal*. (November 2001): 67.

Cull, Frank. "Father Mychal Judge." *World of Hibernia Magazine*. Winter 2001, 96.

Evans, Sid. "The Brotherhood—Ten thousand men are ready to save your life at any cost. Think about it." *Men's Journal*. (November 2001): 21.

Hanson, Victor Davis. "What Made Them Do Their Duty?—At the Twin Towers, cops and fireman showed they really were New York's Finest, New York's Bravest." *City Journal*. (Autumn 2001): 84-89. This article is one of the best.

Samuels, David. "The Defiant Ones—One moment of resolve that inspired the Nation." *Men's Journal*. (November 2001): 93.

Sides, Hampton. "The Chaplain—The Reverend Mychal Judge was not afraid of the front lines." *Men's Journal.* (November 2001): 77.

Smith, Dennis. "On Holy Ground." *World of Hibernia Magazine.* Winter 2001, 94.

_____. "On the Shoulders of Giants." *World of Hibernia Magazine.* Winter 2001, 82.

BOOKS

Boucher, Michael L., Gary R. Urbanowicz, and Frederick B. Melahn, Jr., *The Last Alarm—The History and Tradition of Supreme Sacrifice in the Fire Departments of New York City.* Evansville, IN: M.T. Publishing Company, Inc. 2006.

Boyle, Kevin. *Braving the Waves—Rockaway Rises ...and Rises Again.* Scotts Valley, CA: Rising Star Press, 2002.

Brotherhood. Introduction by Frank McCourt. New York: American Express Publishing Corporation, 2001.

Burns, Phil. *... bringing everybody home.* Dover, NH: DMC Books, 2009.

_____. *Laughter, Tears & Muffled Drums.* Dover, NH: DMC Books, 2003.

Daly, Michael. *Book of Mychal: The Surprising Life and Heroic Death of father Mychal Judge.* New York: Saint Martin's Press, 2008.

Downey, Tom. *The Last Men Out—Life on the Edge at Rescue 2 Firehouse.* New York: Henry Holt and Company, 2004. Tom Downey is a nephew of Battalion Chief Ray Downey.

Dwyer, Jim, and Kevin Flynn. *102 Minutes—The Untold Story of the Fight to Survive Inside the Twin Towers*. New York: Times Books, Henry Holt and Company LLC., 2005.

FDNY 2001- 2011: A Decade of Remembrance and Resilience. Evansville, IN: M.T. Publishing, Inc., 2011.

Fontana, Marian. *A Widow's Walk—A Memoir of 9/11*. New York: Simon & Schuster, 2005.

Fuentes, Alfredo, with Donald MacLaren, and Helen Morrissey Rizzuto. *American by Choice—One Man's Journey*. Island Park, NY: Fire Dreams Publishing Co. 2004.

Ganci, Chris. *Chief—the Life of Peter J. Ganci, a New York City Firefighter*. New York: Orchard Books, 2003.

Golway, Terry. *So Others Might Live—A History of New York's Bravest the FDNY from 1700 to the Present*. New York: Basic Books, 2002.

Halberstam, David. *Firehouse*. New York: Hyperion, 2002.

Hashagen, Paul, edited by Janet Kimmerly. *The Bravest—An Illustrated History 1865—2002*. Paducah, KY: Turner Publishing, 2002.

In the Line of Duty—A Tribute to New York's Finest and Bravest. Forewords by Bernard B. Kerik and Thomas Von Essen. New York: Regan Books/HarperCollins Publishers, 2001.

Locke, Jessica. *Rescue at Engine 32*. n.p.: n.p., 2007.

O'Sullivan, Shawn, Editor. Essays by Patrice O'Shaughnessy. *New York's Bravest—Eight Decades of Photographs from the Daily News*. New York: pH powerHouse Books, 2002.

Picciotto, Richard. *Last Man Down—A Firefighter's Story of Survival and Escape from the World Trade Center*. New York: A Berkley Book, 2002.

Salka, John, with Barret Neville. *First In, Last Out—Leadership Lessons from the New York Fire Department*. New York: Portfolio, 2004. John Salka's book is a management and leadership book. It contains some 9/11 related material.

Sheridan, Kerry. *Bagpipe Brothers—The FDNY Band's True Story of Tragedy, Mourning, and Recovery*. New Brunswick, NJ, and London: Rutgers University Press, 2004.

Shukwit, Geralyn. *What I Had To Do—Firehouse Photographs, Sept.-Oct. 2001*. Detroit, Chicago and San Francisco: J. Walter Thompson, 2002.

Smith, Dennis. *Report from Ground Zero—The Story of the Rescue Efforts at the World Trade Center*. New York: Viking, 2002.

Spak, Steve. *Mayday! Mayday! Mayday!—The Day The Towers Fell*. New York: Xlibris, 2003. Steve Spak is an Associate Court Clerk in Brooklyn Civil Court. He is the preeminent photographer of New York City fire scenes.

Suson, Gary. *Requiem—Images of Ground Zero*. New York: Barnes & Noble Books, 2002.

Von Essen, Thomas. *Strong of Heart—Life and Death in the Fire Department of New York*. Regan Books/Harper Collins Publishers, 2002.

Wicklund, Jared, Editor. *Fallen Heroes—A Tribute From Fire Engineering*. Tulsa, OK: PennWell, 2001.

FILMS

The Bravest Team: The Rebuilding of the FDNY Football Club.

Brotherhood: Life in the FDNY. Dir. Lilibet Foster. 2004. DVD.

Brothers ... On Holy Ground. Dir. Mike Lennon. Vanguard Cinema, 2003. DVD.

The Guys. Dir. Jim Simpson. Universal Studios, 2003. This film is a drama starring Anthony LaPaglia and Sigourney Weaver. It captures the emotional impact of 9/11 on the FDNY perfectly. Many members of the FDNY were used in the final scene of the film. DVD.

New York Firefighters—the Brotherhood of September 11th. Dir. Peter Schnall. Discovery Channel, 2002. VHS.

9/11. Dir. Jules Naudet, Gedeon Naudet, and James Hanlon. Paramount Home Video, 2002. DVD.

Saint of 9/11—The True Story of Father Mychal Judge. Dir. Glenn Holsten. Hart Sharp Video, 2006. DVD.

Twin Towers. Bill Guttentag, and Robert David Port, Directors. Universal Home Entertainment, 2004. DVD. The twin towers in this case are the Vigiano brothers.

WTC 9-11-01—Day of Disaster. Steve Spak. This is an on-the-scene film without audio, shot minutes after the towers collapsed. DVD

SONGS

De Vale, Brian. "New York's Damn Bravest." Ti Tra Li Productions, 2001.

Griffin, Marian. "Tallon of the Ten House." Truetone, Inc., 2002.

Kellar, Christine. "Terence McShane." Dubway Studios, 2006. This CD features the band *Too Blue*, and Aidan McShane on electric bass, and Kieran McShane on drums.

Otway, Lorcan. "Remember they are with us." Sorcha Dorcha, 2001.

NOTES

[1] Two weeks later, Deputy Commissioner Feehan and Chief Ganci would die in the line of duty. Later still, their names would occupy a place on the newly expanded wall.

[2] Twenty-one Chief Officers would die in the line of duty on September 11.

[3] Bill Groneman, *Battlefields of Texas*, (Plano, TX: Republic of Texas Press, 1997). I have had some success in writing about Texas History.

[4] Al's story is dramatically told in, Alfredo Fuentes, with Donald MacLaren and Helen Morrissey Rizzuto, *American By choice—One Man's Journey*, (Island Park, NY: Fire Dreams Publishing, 2004).

[5] These are important in case of a building collapse, or some other catastrophic occurrence, such as a member missing at a fire. A roll call can be conducted based on the names on the form. If the officer and/or his or her whole company are missing, others can get the information from the copy in the apparatus to aid them in the search. All FDNY companies have a prescribed position and assignment at a fire based on the type of building, how the company is due at the box (what order they are assigned to the alarm), and as to the type of company (engine, ladder, rescue, etc.) If a firefighter is missing at a fire, a calculated guess can be made as to where he or she should have been based on their position or tool assignment on the BF-4. In the case of an engine company like 308, the officer is listed first, then right below, the engine company chauffeur. The riding positions for the remaining members are nozzle, back-up, door, and control. Since we had no apparatus or

even tools for that matter it was not necessary to include all this information.

[6] The gear is very good protection at a fire but it is cumbersome. It is also controversial. There is the danger of over extending oneself in a fire and going in further that one ordinarily would have. There is also the danger of over heating with the gear on. The FDNY had to revamp its fire fighting procedures based on this, utilizing earlier and more frequent relief of units working at a fire.

[7] The helmet is important not only for protection but for identification. A unit's company number is on the front piece of the helmet. Firefighters' front pieces have their company number and their badge number on them. Their front pieces are also color coded to indicate the type of units they are assigned: Engine—black; Ladder—red; Rescue—blue; Squad—yellow; Marine—green. Officers' front pieces are white, regardless of the type of unit. My front piece had "308" in black in the middle. Above that were two trumpets indicating that I was the captain of an engine company. Below the 308 was a black strip with the word "Captain" in white. Four of the five guys with me could be identified by the white "308" on their black front pieces. Only Ralph Scerbo's was different. He had a black front piece with "Battalion Aide," and "Battalion 51" on it. We were about to go into complete chaos and I was concerned about getting separated from my guys and/or losing someone. The helmets provided instant recognition of one's company members.

[8] His brother, Warren Haring, had been a young firefighter in Ladder Company 6, where my father had worked, in Chinatown, to the northeast of where we stood. I had gone to Fire Marshal school with Warren back in

1981. He had already been promoted to Fire Marshal and I was promoted soon thereafter. We even worked a tour or two as partners in the Fire Marshals Red Cap Task Force.

[9] Normally at a cellar fire the first due engine company (us in this case) would go around to the back or side of the building and go into the cellar through an exterior door and extinguish the fire. At that time, the second due engine would go into the front door, keep the interior cellar door closed and safeguard the hallway and stairs by preventing the fire from extending up the stairs. Unfortunately, one of the first due ladder company members who had gone around the rear of the building told Capt. Higgins that there was no exterior cellar door (actually, there was). Higgins decided that we had to go in on the first floor open the interior cellar door, and attack down the cellar stairway with the hose line. So, there we went.

This was easier said than done since, when Ladder Company 175 popped the interior cellar door open, the doorway and whole cellar stairway became one solid tunnel of flame. I opened the line but the stream had no appreciable affect on the fire. The cellar right below us was fully involved in flame and now the fire was seeking its only path upward through the open cellar door. I was told later by our engine company chauffeur, Pete Keiser, that the bushes outside were bursting into flame due to the heat from the cellar windows.

Capt. Higgins kept yelling at me to shut the line down. Every time I did the flames would get worse and push us back toward the front door. Meanwhile, someone found the exterior cellar entrance and an engine company began to push in from that direction. A thing you don't want to happen at a fire was what was happening at that moment—

two opposing hose lines pushing the fire at one another. The first blast knocked us right out the front door. We recovered quickly and got back down the narrow hallway to the inferno at the cellar door. My back ended up against a radiator which was red hot from the fire below, and the stairwell walls began to burn through to the hallway. Higgins held me in place with the line going. I ran out of air in my tank, and finally yelled "I'm starting to burn!" He grabbed me, threw me out of the way, and put Joe Hands on the nozzle. I crawled out of the hallway after losing my helmet. I later ended up going to the hospital with burns to my ears. Higgins used up Joe and then threw the door man, Steve Filipelli, on the nozzle.

It was a wild fire. We never did get down the cellar stairs until the fire was knocked down from below. A civilian died in the cellar and it took a long time to find his body since everything became a uniform black and there was a foot of water on the floor.

I got back from the hospital some hours later and found Capt. Higgins sitting in the kitchen. I asked him why he kept telling me to shut down the nozzle. He said he wanted to shut down so we would be able to dive down the stairs and fight the fire from the cellar. Luckily we did not do this. It would have been like going down a chimney with a roaring fire in the fireplace. We would have been killed.

[10] Engine 332 was later moved to a new firehouse on Bradford Street and shared quarters there with Ladder 175.

[11] For more on Chief Ganci see, Chris Ganci, *Chief— The Life of Peter J. Ganci, A New York City Firefighter*, (New York: Orchard Books, 2003).

[12] The members of Engine 238 were in the lobby of Tower One when Tower Two collapsed. They all got out

but Lieutenant Glenn Wilkinson returned to search for a member he thought was missing. He died in the collapse of Tower One.

[13] The old Three-Nine (39th) Battalion was comprised of Engines 332, 236, 290, 225 and Ladders 103 and 107. Engine 290 is quartered with Ladder 103 on Sheffield Avenue, Brooklyn. You would have a hard time finding a crazier bunch than the Sheffield Ave. crew from the late 1970s. For many years they were the busiest companies in Brooklyn and always in the top five in the city. Their insignia "POSA" stands for "Prides of Sheffield Avenue," but it also derives from the name of a former member, Frank Posa. I worked in their companies a number of times as a firefighter on overtime and on details

[14] Our fathers, Bill Groneman and Ernie Esposito were New York City Firemen (this was before the term "firefighter" was adopted). The two often saw one another at morning Mass in Our Lady of Grace Church in Howard Beach before going to work at their respective firehouses. They did not know one another at the time but would say hello since they knew each other was "on the job." One such meeting occurred on July 14, 1956. Later that evening a fire broke out in the Wanamaker Store in Manhattan. The store consisted of two eighty-year-old, five-story buildings, covering an entire city block. The fire, fought by eight hundred firemen, raged for two days. Two hundred forty firemen were either injured or suffered smoke inhalation. One of those rendered unconscious by the smoke, and then dragged into the street, was Bill Groneman. When he came to he looked to his side and found Ernie Esposito, also injured, lying next to him. Ernie looked over and said, "You should have prayed harder!" They became lifelong

friends after that. Bill Groneman was a fireman in Ladder Company 6 at the time of his death in 1980. Ernie Esposito retired from the FDNY as a Captain.

[15] In order to understand this it takes a little understanding of the somewhat complicated work schedule of the FDNY. The normal schedule is divided up into twenty-five group numbers. When a person is assigned to a fire company he or she is put in a certain group number. Six of these groups are listed on the calendar for working a day tour (9x6) and six for a night tour (6x9). The numbers on the calendar tell you when you are scheduled to work. If you are working according to this schedule in the FDNY, it is referred to as "working the chart." A "set of tours" consists of one's scheduled day tours and night tours. A normal set of tours consists of working two day tours in a row, having off forty-eight hours, working two night tours in a row, and then having off seventy-two hours. Then, the whole process starts over again. After every third repeat of this sequence you have seventy-two hours off after your day tours, instead of forty-eight hours. This is to adjust the hours so that it all averages out to a forty-hour work week at the end of the year. It is rare that anyone works their regular tours any more. Most work a mutual exchange of tours ("mutuals" in FDNY parlance). One swaps with his or her opposite number on the chart so one works twenty-four hours straight and then is off for seventy-two hours. Most of these twenty-four hour tours start and end at 6 p.m. It works out that every fourth one starts and ends at 9 a.m.

[16] With a simple name last name like "Day" you would not think that there would be too much material for firehouse nicknames, but that was not the case. Jimmy was known on Bradford Street as "Otis," for the black singing

group in the movie *Animal House*, "Otis Day and the Knights." Some of the more creative guys also nicknamed him after a line from the song "Camptown Races," calling him "Oh dee do dah Day!"

[17] Once, when "TK" was assigned the roof position, he decided not to wait for the ladder company chauffeur to raise the aerial ladder and then climb it. Instead he clung to the tip of the ladder while it was still bedded on the apparatus and then had the chauffeur raise the ladder. A safety chief would have had a nervous breakdown if on the scene.

TK was also part of a fringe group of mad scientists in the firehouse. One night they decided to disconnect one of the gas jets of the kitchen stove, fill a large, black plastic garbage bag with the lighter-than-air flammable gas. They closed it, brought it out into the backyard, where TK tied a long line of toilet paper to the bag. He lit the paper with a match and launched the bag while the flame ate its way up. A fiery explosion lighted the night sky over East New York. It did not go unnoticed since at least one civilian from up on Highland Boulevard rushed to the firehouse to report the explosion.

[18] Their firehouse lost the following members on September 11, 2001: Lieutenants Vincent Giammona and Michael Warchola, Firefighters Louis Arena, Andrew Brunn, Thomas Hannafin, Paul Keating, John Santore, and Gregory Saucedo, all of Ladder 5; Battalion Chiefs William McGovern, Richard Prunty, and Firefighter Faustino Apostol, Jr., all of Battalion 2, which shares quarters with Engine 24 and Ladder 5.

[19] Jules Naudet, Gedeon Naudet, and James Hanlon, *9/11* (Paramount Home Video, 2002), DVD.

[20] Josephine Harris passed away in January, 2011, at age sixty-nine.

[21] This information is taken from photocopies of Engine 308's company journal for Saturday, September 15, 2001. The details of the changes in assignments are recorded in my handwriting. The uncertainty about who the fifth firefighter assigned to duty with Engine 308 at 12:45 p.m. is due to the fact that the right-hand side of the page did not fall within the field of the photocopy.

[22] Engine Company 10 lost Lieutenant Gregg Atlas and Firefighters Jeffrey Olsen and Paul Pansini. Ladder Company 10 lost Lieutenant Stephen Harrell (Battalion 7, covering in L 10), Firefighter Sean Tallon, and retired Captain James Corrigan.

[23] See Bill Guttentag, and Robert David Port, Directors, *Twin Towers* (Universal Home Entertainment, 2004), DVD.

[24] Chief Burns has two excellent books on his Fire Department experiences. See Phil Burns, *Laughter, Tears, & Muffled Drums*, (Dover, NH: DMC Books, 2003); and, *... bringing everybody home*, (Dover, NH: DMC Books, 2009).

[25] At the time of completing this memoir I opened a plastic storage bin in which I had place some material related to September 11, 2001, and which I had not opened since then. Among a few items I found the small athletic bag I had carried. In it was a folding knife I had long since given up as lost, a flashlight, some work gloves, a shirt, and a jar of Vicks Vapo-Rub. I could not understand why I had this item, and then I remembered. It was to apply under my nose while working at the site to mask the odor of other things.

[26] This passage on Ronan Tynan was written on Saint Patrick's Day, March 17, 2011.

[27] See Dennis Smith, *Report From Ground Zero*, (New York: Viking, 2002).

[28] Chief Salka later published a book on management and leadership. See John Salka, with Barret Neville, *First In, Last Out—Leadership Lessons from the New York Fire Department* (New York: Portfolio, 2004).

[29] Smith, *Report From Ground Zero*, 274.

[30] Battalion Chief Art Lakiotes, Safety Command, New York City Fire Department, *World Trade Center Task Force interview of Firefighter Timothy Brown*, January 15 2002, on www.thebravest.com. Also see Mike Lennon, *Brothers ... On Holy Ground*, (Vanguard Cinema, 2003), DVD.